ROSES IN
THE LEMON TREE

life's paradoxes

Printed in the United States of America
Published May 2023

Editor: Gail Riena Michael
Cover Illustration: Jerry Downs

ISBN paperback: 979-8-9880643-0-5
ISBN ebook: 979-8-9880643-1-2

In Praise of "Roses In The Lemon Tree"

Rev. Patty Truman powerfully reminds us that thankfulness for the sweetness of life *is an acquired skill. While modern life tempts us to rush blindly ahead, she suggests we learn to "metabolize pain as energy, trusting again the life work we do." Patricia guides us to a deep well of understanding where we learn to know ourselves.*

— **Liane Brouillette** / Professor, School of Education, University of California, Irvine

Patricia Truman's poems are relatable and speak of the need to slow down, be mindful, and in quietness to sense all that is around us. It is a sacred exercise to soothe, heal and nurture ourselves. Her poems comforted and filled me with joy.

— **Dr. George Chandy** BBS, PhD / Writer and Professor Emeritus, School of Medicine, University of California Irvine

This book is a metaphysical treatise on the condition of one's prayerful, insightful and inspired thoughts. Glimmers of transcendentalism pervade with a beautiful promise. The gentle guidance for readers to participate in this discovery is imperative for a successful conclusion.

— **Bonnie Holt** / Mother, Joyous Grandmother, Artist, Homemaker, Gardener

In our world of growing uncertainty, Patricia Truman's poetry takes us to the realm of mysticism and gives golden wings to our imagination.

— **Sukhdev Dail** PhD / International Sculptor, Painter and Teacher. Former art director for Universal, Hanna-Barbera, MGM and other Hollywood studios. His works are in museums and galleries around the world. sdail@comcast.net

I have been Rev. Patricia Truman's student, teacher, friend, and active sister of her Soul Family for many years. From Sacred Circle to enlightening dinner conversations on healing this planet. I'm forever grateful and continually inspired by her wisdom, grace, and magical poetry which I use as a tool to enlighten and uplift many yoga students and clients.

— **Carolyn Long** / Quantum Healer, International Yoga Teacher, Quality Life Coach *"Aspire to inspire before you expire!"*

Roses In The Lemon Tree *is joyous and gleeful reading. Each poem's bud continues to open every time you reflect on the words.*

— **Ruben Flores** / Vision Scape, International Designer
and Owner of Laguna Nursery

Patricia Truman's poetic words create a masterpiece for the heart. Her works shift our perspective and give us hope. With each new book, she continues to surprise and astound.

— **Gail Michael** / Editor and Published Author, *Unveiling Rosanna*

I was deeply moved by the poem Mystic Cloud Walker *in your book with that title. It brought up so many memories and feelings of the great women in my life—mother, friends, wife and others. Heartfelt thanks!*

— **Lee Van Slyke** / Consultant

Each time I opened, reflected and took a few more steps with you, I pictured you praying over Mystic Cloud Walker *as you held one end of your book and I the other. I was moved to read aloud —connect deeply, emotionally, alchemically—with each word, question, reflection, and mood. I was touched by your feminine humanness, connection to nature and the Divine, and sense of purpose to impart your life's wisdom to your family's next generations as well as to your wider human family.*

— **Veronique Marchal** / Founder & Creative Impact Officer,
"Me We Action" | www.andactionagency.com

I enjoyed reading Mystic Cloud Walker, *particularly "Wild Woman," "The Mode of Transportation for Our Earth," and "I Know Who You Are." Your new title,* Roses In The Lemon Tree, *really appealed to me.*

— **Bill Giovinazzo** / Author and Public Speaker | https://italianita.blog/

Patricia Truman weaves with her poetry a magic carpet ride of thoughtfully chosen, beautiful words ...

— **Al Blake** / "Old School" Blues Musician
and owner and designer of Sunstone Gardens

ROSES IN
THE LEMON TREE

life's paradoxes

PATRICIA PEPER TRUMAN

dedication

Roses In My Mother's Lemon Tree

She was a natural redhead with freckles to prove the genuineness of her dark, rich chestnut hair. She was elegant, a lady well-educated and in love with words, books, and people. She had a vivid imagination as well as being highly intuitive. She lived in the 20th century. She was my mother and she often spoke of the book she would write one day, but never did...at least not on paper.

She did write indelibly on the hearts and minds of her family who lovingly called her Tutu, a nickname she was given on a cruise to Hawaii that was gifted by my grandmother after my father died by his own hand. But that was long ago and another story. The book that floated tenderly in her mind was to be called "Roses In The Lemon Tree."

She has of late, intuitively let me know that it is my legacy to write such a book, now mine. I understand her metaphor that life at times seems like a lemon-laden tree, yet intertwined with life's branches are roses, lovely, fragrant roses.

We had such a tree and vine in the small yard upon which our beach cottage sat in a friendly neighborhood lined with other bungalows and a handful of new homes. The street had the Catholic Church at its helm and the Pacific Ocean at its stern and was in one of the loveliest places on the planet,

Laguna Beach, California. It was a locale where both lemons and roses grew in abundance.

So, roses and lemons shall be discovered in this reflective collection of prose, poetry, meditative writings, and memoirs. I trust it will bear a gift for each one who may pick it up and read even a small portion.

Dedicated to that dear lady of many names: Elizabeth, Red Peper, Mrs. Wesley Peper, and later in life, Mrs. Alan Ferguson. To my friends one and all, she was Mom. To her friends, she was Liz. To the grandchildren and finally to almost all of us, she was Tutu.

We all loved you, hopefully, well.

contents

chapter 3 — LISTENING IS A SILENT FORCE

chapter 4 — EARTH'S BOUNTIFUL GIFTS

chapter 5 — SOULFUL SEA

chapter 6 — MYSTERIES

chapter 7 — MYSTICAL MOMENTS

chapter 8 — THE LIGHT AND ALL THAT IS

chapter 9 — HOLY EXPECTATIONS

chapter 1

Roses & Lemons

PRAYERFUL TRIBUTE FOR MY MOTHER

The Great Hubble Telescope pictures inspiring
    and stirring something far deeper within my soul
Hubble eye suggests the all-seeing eye,
    The Infinite gaze ever aware from the expansive
    inclusive
original compassionate consciousness
    Omnipresent, omnipotent
Omni-immensity resident in all living things

Everything in the Cosmos is alive, moving multiple
molecules
    each cell serving, dying, born anew constantly
The Great Creator is ever eternally creating from the vast
    magnificent source of the infinite beingness
into every expression of life that has ever been
    and shall ever be.

A humble dedication of my offering
    to this monumental, magnificent light
Illuminating Heaven, Earth, and each particle of
    Creation

May this volume touch, move and perhaps inspire those
    who chose to partake herein
with sincerity that each shall be enriched
    Blessings always —

Patricia Peper Truman, Roses In The Lemon Tree

ROSES IN THE LEMON TREE OF LIFE

I must stop and remember
        When life becomes overwhelming
That experience often brings forth
        Roses in the lemon tree

When the tides come washing in
        With the velocity of a raging storm
That place within
        Recalls there are roses in the lemon tree

With life, there is also death
        With sorrow, also joy
Gaining a perspective to view the journey
        And see the roses in the lemon tree

Love visits and sometimes goes on its way
        Passions ebb and flow
Nothing is forever; all is in flux
        Like the roses in the lemon tree

winter comes and the flowers die away
        The dormancy of skeleton shapes invades
Then comes spring carrying new life
        Budding roses in the lemon tree

Seasons slither into years
        Days mount like giant monuments
To the passage of time, until there is no more
        Blooming still are the roses in the lemon tree

METAPHORICAL LEMONS AND ROSES

As varied as are roses and equally individualized lemons,
        so are the inner voices sharing practical prompts or
a helpful directive, also, a deep mystical occasional
voice relaying
        cosmic glimpses into the elemental ethers

There are others presenting a collection of soft poetic
voices inspiring
        both prose and poetry
a deeply personal voice whispering messages
for the listener's
        receptive ears alone

Every now and again a whimsical voice of a lighter even
sassy tone
        There are countless ones always present to the
        faithful and
prayerfully hearts request to the holy presence
        They or "We" as they identify themselves to this writer,
        are whispering
immediately in my quiet, awaiting, and open sensing.

The blessings of the Divine are fresh and new every moment
        just as the infinite life force is always flowing
        through every
living thing creating each unique and lovely rose, as well as
every lemon,
        each a similar but not exact size, shape or tastiness

Roses nourish our deep soul self-responding to beauty
 Our precious bodies rejoice at the nutritious
vitamin C in lemon's juice, a wedge in water, delicious
  fresh salad dressing or savory sauce

All these gifts come from two single seeds—
 A lemon seed and a rose hip grown with skillful hands
Roses, lemons, poetry and prose uniquely brought forth
 to open receptive vessels
Both are gifts from the divine intelligence as ongoing
expressions
 of the Creator's love

THE START OF ALL THINGS

How does anything that lives come into being?
What life force brings all that is seen, into view?
How is the process discovered, learned, and used?
    Ahh, the hidden is exposed and revealed

A seed is the initial source of everything that is
revealing itself through the universal mind
Seeds are dropped into fertile awaiting consciousness
    The inspired seed is accepted, first mental actions taken

A cherished seed is carefully planted into the ground
tending and nurturing, water, sun and air, working together
First explosion beneath the earth, and a tender green shoot
spirals upward
    The embedded truth within the seed slowly reveals itself

Is it to be a mighty tree, a flower, stalk of celery or untold
other secrets?
The seed is the source of what will be brought into the world
Choosing the right seed is the diligent work of the beholder
    weed or wheat, fruit, flower or poison the choice
    of the planter

What is true for the farm or garden is true for the
industrial world
Concept seeds are plentiful but worthy seeds are more rare
Life affirming implementations for all humankind are
especially precious
    an invention, medical procedure, device, or vaccine

The strength of an idea, can change the entire course
of humankind—
transportation, communication, food sources, clean water
All from a fertile idea, tested, retested bringing life
enriching results
        profiting many, creating jobs, convenience, ease,
        or better health

The reverse is also true, an evil seed of destruction
and mayhem
creating power over others, increasing greed, misery,
or suffering
These seeds not discarded but taken for nefarious motives
        putting humanity and the planet's survival at risk

A lemon seed creates a generously baring yellow
orbed nutrient
A rose seed can produce a vine or bush of many lovely colors
depending upon the secret divinely hidden within the
seed itself
growing, perfuming, in a lovely display
        of roses in the lemon tree

All seeds have come forth from the originality of all there is
Creation itself has brought into being a myriad of fertile
infinite seeds
to be used for wellbeing of all living things—humans, plants
        animals, and the beautiful elements of the earth.
        Seeds are sacred, loving gifts to be used to enrich
        all Creation

EXPECT THE UNEXPECTED

Ahh, the paradox of the unexpected in life should be expected
That which is your plan is often thwarted
The olde saying perhaps is true,
    "The best laid plans of mice and men are soon to go awry"

Flights are missed and nimble one must be
To rant and rave is of no avail
To accept, learn a precautionary lesson is a goodly practice
    "Would of, could of, should of" are useless in
      unexpected moments

Flexibility is the skill to reflect asking for the lesson
An exercise to humbly be embraced
Those inquiries can shed insights but for now, acceptance is
the balm
    "Only change is constant," a true paradoxical saying

An unexpected blow can evoke expanding perspectives
In the scheme of things, ask "How important is it?"
Use a mantra to defuse one's internal desire to explode into
    various unpleasant emotions
    Breathe deeply, exhale slowly, all is well

Daydream, a better moment.

LIFE HAS ROSES AND LEMONS

Life has roses and lemons
    Do not be overly focused on either, overwrought
    or engaged
        but be grateful, for both carry a portion of life's
        experience

Even the great teachers had annoyances while existing in
earthly kingdom
    at such a moment they sourced the wise creator's
    assistance
        thus, so can we

The Great One lived an example of how a human has
resources
    beyond the obvious allowing the Divine Unseen forces
    to guide,
        to help with loving assistance, to work on
        our behalf
            where we cannot affect desired results

Those spiritually attuned, possess more interdependency
just as a
    working cooperative builds relationship in the
    human realm
        None of us are alone except by our own being
        closed to anything
            except our own self-important capabilities

Great stubborn pride or disbelief blocks the flow ever
available and awaiting
　　to assist, help, guide any who call onto a path not
　　fraught with upsets,
　　　　defeats or the meaningless belief of bad luck

Luck is a random roll of the dice putting faith or hope upon
something beyond
　　ourselves over which we have no say or
　　so-called control
　　　　rather than believing within is an
　　　　interconnected working
　　　　　　respectful relationship with the ever-
　　　　　　internal spirit

Resident within is mentor, devotee, all loving hands wanting
the highest good
　　to come forth in this moment if we but call upon
　　Higher Helper to assist
　　　　with ease and good results for all, thus to allow
　　　　being in the flow
　　　　　　of yet unknown as to time and means
　　　　　　　　is this not faith by surrender
　　　　　　　　and acceptance of
　　　　　　　　　　both lemons and roses?

THE LIFE FORCE

Loving the touch of tough leathery leaves
    with dainty orchid flowers
There is such strength in this plant
    it seems to grow in a matter of hours

The life force in my garden
    is my constant delight
The springing forth of new growth
    popping from brown earth into sight

Harvesting sweet pea seeds
    early this Sunday morning
The promise of future beauty
    in little round black seed born

The cycle of life all about us
    birth, growth, blossoming then dying
A message repeated, again and again
    a dance danced without trying

Being only an observer
    of the magnificent mysteries
But in the observation
    Learning one's own intricacies

Do we not conceive an idea or dream
      birthed, nurtured, blossom and die?
The cycles within one's own life
      seasons upon which we can rely
Every life has winter
      cold, deadening and bleak
The season of frozen in place
      afraid to think or speak

Then comes the thaw of a new idea
      the shift begins, the trickle then flow
At last, winter is breaking up
      the idea we dreamed we begin to know

GIFT OF LEMONS AND ROSES –
A METAPHOR FOR LIFE

Lemons are associated with tart, sour, something
to be sweetened
>   Truly, many lemons are relatively sweet, flavorful,
>   a healthy fruit
>>   filled with Vitamin C, added to water, salad
>>   dressings, fish
>>>   and the old well known wise adage:
>>>   *"If life serves you lemons,*
>>>   *make lemonade"*

The underlying message to sweeten up the unpleasant
occurrences
>   or tell a new story from an old worn out long
>   lamented tale
>>   Re-frame an internalized picture that no longer
>>   serves you
>>>   Freshen, see the lesson or wisdom as a gift
>>>   moving on to be now a wiser human

Roses ah, roses, the universal sign of romance, beauty, love
>   Roses come in countless colors, shades, shapes, sizes
>>   some emit perfume, others just robust beauty
>>>   Others do both and seem to delight
>>>   the heart
>>>>   captured in many forms of art

So is life! Filled with situations at times that appear
like lemons,
    yet a lemon is not bad; just needs to be
    used appropriately
        When we learn to not react but inspect
        for a learning clue
            then the roses intertwined in
            every experience
                bud, then bloom giving beauty
                before unseen

Look for the roses, perhaps even a thorn hidden from sight
    enjoy the gifts bearing richness into your heart mind
        Let us not dislike lemons but find the benefit
        carried therein
            for the great, loving Creator has given
            us both
                to expand awareness, finding
                a hidden gem

A gem once given is forever our own to carry as
a precious award
    for overcoming of despair to delight, or healing
    from wounds,
        Many forms of tribulations once conquered,
        now a prize
            that becomes the jewel of the heart carrying
                light illuminating out into
                our Universe

The great green gardens of the world as well as the wee
cottage plots of delight
        are all labors of love that parade before welcoming eyes
                displaying their beauty, fruitage, and purpose
                        just like us

Is a garden not a grand metaphor for life?
        Those lovingly cared for thrive
                contributing to the joy of sharing desired fruit
                        those abused, ignored, unattended
                                shrivel and slowly disappear
                                        sadly, denying their precious
                                        potential gift to life

GIFT OF NOW

Time is cascading by tumbling down the cliffs of eternity
Each breath is present, past and the ever-occurring future
The linear expanse of all there has ever been
  this moment and what it will be
    yet it is all a continuum of conscious evolution

We are living in a holographic Universe
Everything contained in everything that is or will be
Like a drop of ocean water containing all its composition
  the essence of all present therein, microbes
  and ancient
    mammoths, included in its present chemistry

Each breath holds all of life
Ever forming and re-forming as are all living things
Everything being constantly created and recreated
automatically
  every human breathes in all others from this
  air soup of
    discarded dead cells, hair, and skin particles

A paradoxical intricacy of creation, a puzzle for our
logical minds
This moment's inhale contains dinosaurs, diamonds,
stardust, soot
And pollen circulating around the globe
  such a magical carousel we all are riding,
  celebrating the
    powerful wonder of all that exists in this precious
    gift of Now

SHARING AND CARING

All living things require care
    the acquired skill of graceful
Sharing and caring appreciated by
    roses and lemons, babies, and teen
Adults and those much more mature
    all need carefully chosen loving nourishment

Being prompted, this quiet cool morning
    to feed flowers, roses, and fruit trees
An act of tending denoting caring, thus sharing
    in proper season, the nutrients having reached roots
Building wellbeing, vital and alive
    will reward with luscious gifts

Beauty in the form of ample blossoms and buds
    exhibited the law of fair exchange
So, it is with great granddaughter, we now reside together
    learning to nourish and care for her carefully
Like a new dance partner melding into each other's rhythm
    and pace, an unspoken communication

Becoming harmonious, in step with each other's
anticipating needs
    the joy of participating in the excitement of youth
A first work experience, new locale and her adjusting of
being with
    GrandPatty 24/7, 365, a mutual challenging,
    rewarding learning curve
Just as life — becoming familiar and knowledgeable
    with the needs of the person with whom we are with

Tasks including garden, home, and one's work expression
    family, friends, associates, students, clients
The dailiness honing skills of being sensitive to it all
    the sweet divine creative life energy prompts, whispers
Guides humans, plants, animals, and all living things
    such a glorious participatory adventure of sharing
    and caring!

ROSES

A rose, so lovely
Bud and thorn
Green leaves
My fingers scorn

Petals opening
Perfume released
From bud so tight
Magnificence unleashed

Petals in full glory
Spent, begin to fade
And slowly drop
Scattered in the shade

The glory has gone
Yet a secret remains
Not finished yet
The hip still reins

The pure essence
The soul seeds tight
Of rose Madonna
Hidden from sight

Vessel expressing there
Forming so slowly
A precious seed
Now comes royally

Seeds are the soul
Expressions life chose
The most precious part
Of vital beauteous rose

LIFE'S PAGES OF BOTH LEMONS AND ROSES

To ignore a part of your past is to tear out pages of your life story. It is like deleting chapters that were meaningful, painful, happy, and sad. Not wanting to remain where once you were seemingly pleased to be, is not a reason to obliterate what was, pretending that person or experience no longer has value or meaning.

We all write our life stories in our daily lives – page by page, line by line; relationship by relationship we forge ourselves. To the capacity that we are able to love is the dimension to which we can expand. Refusing to love or feel deeply causes contraction and restriction that narrows the life and shrinks the soul.

Narrow minds from the beginning of time destroyed written records. Burning books, why? Fear of the deeper wisdom within that evokes feelings that do not want to be awakened. The mind wants to reject what the heart already knows. So, burn those books telling the lies that prick one's soul and thinking the wisdom is gone. In that form yes, but truth has a way of finding its way to the surface of a listening heart. It never dies but recedes at times to appear again. So, it is with the experience of human life. You think you can divorce, cut people off, ignore and forget, but there is no forgetting, only denial. In the eons of time, what has been lived, said, expressed and felt reverberates forever in the cosmos, because it remains energetically within the human soul which is eternal and will never die.

The love you once felt is still alive at some level and will not be destroyed. You only delude yourself to think you have cast that part of your life forever away. You have not. What once was always is in the realm of vibratory energy. That energy does not disappear or go away; it only changes form. Honor your life story, the sad and disappointing times as well as the successful and jubilant occasions.

Life is a journey and each step on the road is meaningful for the next. Who we are today is a composite of those with whom we shared our life with yesterday, and who we become will be colored by who we spend time and energy with tomorrow. No chapters missing in the realm of the invisible, every page, each person has written upon the heart, an energy always remaining within us.

PARADOXICAL THINKING –
ROSES IN THE LEMON TREE

What is a paradox?
Something seemingly absurd or self-contradictory,
inconsistent,
Incongruous, anomalous, a statement opposed to common
sense and
      is yet perhaps trusted

A phrase:
can't live with you or without you

Mahatma Gandhi said: *"What you do in life*
may be insignificant but very important you do it"
      Wise but a paradoxical thought

Paradoxical usually involves contradictory or a logical
unacceptable conclusion
yet interrelated elements existing simultaneously, persist
over time,
a saint and yet a sinner, or
      Perhaps our human condition?

Roses don't grow out of the Lemon Tree
yet grow on the tree
Famous people also say often quoted statements
quirky but wise: *"It's weird not to be weird,"*
      ~John Lennon

Pure paradoxical purpose is to arrest attention provoking
fresh thought:
Less is more, or *Selfishness vs selflessness*
Vacillating between two perspectives wanting our own
desires and yet
        sacrificing to please others

Often from religious pundits may feel nice, connected,
or safe, yet a catalyst
pushing us into hole of despair or judging others leading
to feeling
indescribably disconnected, superior or inferior
        We are the only true way, or *Be saved or lost.*

Paradoxical thinking can provoke thinking and examining
our precepts:
Is love a paradox?
Simple and complicated at same time
        Is it absurd or self-contradictory?

Politicians often use statements sounding reasonable
leading to senseless or logically unacceptable conclusion
when examined; also using oxymorons delivering
        an inherent truth contradicting

What we already know with compressed words
        contrary to opinion or expectation

False news or outright lies
Weapons of mass destruction
Spend our way to prosperity

Anonymous sayings in our culture:
      "Do a thing you think you cannot do"
      "Enemy of my enemy is my friend"
      "Damned if you do, damned if you don't"
      "Beginning at the end"
      "Living in the present for the future"
      "Louder you are less you are heard"
      "Impossible is not a word in my vocabulary"
      "Only constant is change"

"If everyone is special, no one is"
A provocative thought!
    ~Walt Disney

"Youth wasted on the young" —
    ~George Bernard Shaw

COME, BELOVED, COME

In the preciousness of this moment, knowing that all are created in the image and likeness of the Divine, hear the mystical beloved speak:

"Dear One, I love you. I have loved you from the very foundation of the Earth. I have loved you since you were first conceived in my Mind and Heart. Come, come now into my deeper presence. Come, my beloved dear one. Warm yourself with my love. Allow my presence to embrace you. Feel the higher frequency of my vibration at the deepest level of your soul.

Did you see my Sun rise this morning? Did you hear its song? I love you. My faithfulness has caused the Sun to rise since the Dawn of Creation. This light is a testimony to my faithful love for you.

Did you see the moon last night?
Did you hear the concerto of love that the moon sings?
I love you. I will never leave you nor forsake you.
I am with you always, forever and ever.

I bring you no small bouquets.
I bring you meadows gloriously alive with flowers.
I bring you majestic mountains, sparkling streams filled with diamonds of light.
I bring you my monumental oceans teeming
with life, vitality supporting the planet with fresh air,

moisture, and sea life.
I bring you forest glen, desert beauty, blue sky,
and clouds that drift painting you a new picture each day.

I bring you sunsets, sunrises, seasons, snow, rain, sunshine,
and incredible beauty.
Do you not hear the songs each sing?
Listen, listen, listen.

I bring you the greatest gift — resurrection and new life.
At any moment, anywhere, for anyone, that which you call
Easter morn is available.
"Yes" is the intention of the heart.
Ever I move Heaven and Earth to touch you,
meet with you and guide your new life.

Come, Beloved, come."

chapter 2

The Hem of Creation

THINGS THAT DELIGHT ME

Flowers so brilliant in my garden
A surprise! A win! A love!
A tender touch, a kind word, a new idea
The sure realization from above

A day with loved ones
The excitement of learning, being, doing
Soft pretty fabrics, a proper outfit
A horse's soft muzzle, music, dancing
Miracles flowing and a lazy sit

The beach water, sun and sand
A child's hand in mine, a hug or a kiss
Travel to many an exotic land
Every second alive, nothing to miss!

A good cup of coffee laced with black strap molasses
in the morning, sitting with my notebook,
time to be with Omnipresent Thee!

A GARDENER OF LIFE TOUCHES
THE HEM OF CREATION

A gardener carefully places a new addition to the
garden tenderly
      plants the small living species into the prepared
      soil bed
            having gently separated its small fragile roots
                  into the waiting new home wrapping it
                        with a rich mixture just right
                        to comfort
                              and allow it to flourish

Like a new parent gazing upon their precious bundle
of potentiality
      so carefully wrapping it in its carefully chosen
      garments and
            special blanket, gazing, dreaming of what
            this infant
                  may become, envisioning wonderful
                  achievements
                      then so responsibly choosing just
                      the right
                          place in the awaiting long
                          ago prepared
                              bassinet, its special nest
                              for now

The Universal Gardener envisions a vision for each soul
lovingly created
    at the dawn of massive movements of planets,
stars, explosions
        and a carefully prepared Earth to be their
        future dwelling
            of belonging for a day or decades, every soul
            to grow their
                roots, flourish, develop according
                to the choices of
                    each individualized heart-mind
                    that takes life
                        on this beautiful planet
                        meant to be

A joy, cared for and nourished for each carefully crafted soul
    having been given gifts, abilities, revelatory
understandings
        as part of the mixture of being a human being
        fully equipped with
            everything needed for life and godliness, to
            flourish or fall,
                rise again, or fall into defeat in accord
                with their own
                    self developed consciousness.

All are given attributes for the journey like any
    good gardener desiring a verdant, successful oasis
        of beauty, bounty contributing to welfare of all

INTERTWINED

Lemons and roses side by side
    responding to the glory of morning new,
        their own special expression
           intertwining cooperating growing daily
              to bring forth the gifts embedded
              in each
                upon creation, a pure promise

Feeling it is so with humans who lived here
    cherished, tended, watered and cared for, these
        and other plants upon a small single plot
        of ground
           in a sleepy quaint beach village; long ago
              a vivid memory of this unusual
              coupling
                remains in my childhood
                memories

The voice of my mother philosophizing
    about roses in the lemon tree
        imprinted this child,
           with the metaphysical
              and deeper symbolism
                carried with me still

Unlike the elders, I grew, and in time, moved away
    my precious parents passed on one at a time
        from this revered plot on our planet

I have never been able to totally release
this sweet cherished, yet quiet,
humble
spot in lovely Laguna Beach

When my days are fully expressed
and sharing of my soul no longer appearing
on the page,
this sacred site of generational memories
shall lovingly be placed for safekeeping,
into the hands of my children
to be shared with expanding
family

There is a special light vibration permeating this tiny dab of
earth sacred to our hearts and minds; again teaching
life has beauty and ugly, sweet and tart,
tears as well as laughter,
opposites seemingly resident
in the human pilgrimage

Yet, held correctly with simple grace,
mindfully creating a life
with beauty and poise
learning from losses and gains,
embracing acceptance of
both lemons and roses in tree of life

IS A GARDEN NOT A METAPHOR FOR LIFE?

The great green gardens of the world
    as well as the wee cottage plots of delight
are all labors of love, that parade before
    welcoming eyes
displaying their beauty, fruitage, and purpose
    just like us

A garden seems a grand metaphor for life
    those lovingly cared for thrive
contributing to the joy of sharing desired fruit
    those abused, ignored, unattended,
shrivel and slowly disappear
    sadly, denying their precious potential gift to life

GARDEN WONDERINGS

Opening the front door to view the day
Breathing great breaths of early morning air
Surveying my small verdant garden giving me great pleasure
What is the pull of the garden,
A feast for my senses

Eyes searching among thousands of leaves for
new appearances
A bud beckoning, a lovely flash of color, as early blossom comes
silently forth celebrating the day; for me it is
a grand adventure
Are the greetings and whispers just below my ability
to hear?
It seems so as if loving utterances come my way, I feel,
but hear not
The garden shows its caring by sharing its beauty, bounty,
fruit and flower

Others enjoy its gifts—family, friends
Those walking by even my helpers are becoming attached to
the display.
Hummingbirds trusting, feeling the love here, build
their amazingly
constructed wee nests to then lay their eggs, hatch and
raise their tiny baby birds
The bees have returned enjoying a bowl of water carefully
left for them
and succulents basking rooting in the shallow vessel

Lizards are my ever-watchful companions; adults and babies call all this their own
My grandson Anthony, who has had large lizards enjoying form of reptiles
He once asked me, "GrandPatty, do they ever come before you and raise up and down on their front legs?"
"Yes they do. That means they are taking ownership over you," I laugh and get that they do seem to have an attitude of male authority
We co-exist nicely

Oh, to see the diva and wee people kingdom
The spirits of nature, tree guardians, angels, who knows what
Sometimes sensing a lovely aura of soft light but never had the gift of deeper sight.
Does it mean they are perhaps the call to the garden, putting fingers in
the earth, pruning and picking, giving deep grounding to my inner being?

I imagine a melodic song being sung as the sun begins kissing each small flower face
The tiny blossoms on the Queen Apricot of the garden singing,
"We are awake, we are here, we bear our gifts of golden sweet orbs soon to come"
What a song, charming chant I can only imagine
The thought makes me happy and feeling embraced cherished at last.
Thank You!

CULTIVATION

A plot of soil concealed
A choice of seeds
Bubbling waters that always flow
This, the internal gardener must know

To be familiar with the ground
To know each seed by name
To recognize living water within
But to not cultivate is a sin

For the ground of being
Must be prepared
The seeds carefully selected
Gently planted and not neglected

It is the cultivation that is the secret
First the planting, then the choice
It is the daily tilling of soil
The spiritual practice loyal

No dancer performs well
Without hours of practice
No athlete plays their best
Unless daily, put to the test

Runners must run
Singers must sing
Writers must write
To bring into sight
So, it is with the internal

The cultivation of the Divine
Every mystic, holy one and saint
Has a spiritual practice not to faint

Love the Lord Divine first
Cultivate the spirit within
Meet each day in quiet time
Prayer, meditation, thus all is thine!

A GARDENING MORNING MEDITATION

Silent stalkers searching through the garden
    Pecking and scratching, a sip of water from
    the fountain
Swinging on the food filled seed holders
    Swivel necks checking constantly for unsafe conditions
Finally investigating feeders wee speckled, plain varieties
of precious little
    birds busy about, hunting and feeding in the early
    morning sunshine
A joyous silent, of so quiet pageantry, the observant scribe
distracted from
    the page to enjoy this small kaleidoscope of life

Birds, budding blooms, and blossoms bursting forth on
a variety of fruit
    trees—apricot, apple, orange, lime, tangerine, plum
    and lemon
Roses all cut and bare sending forth red fresh new leaves
recovering from
    winter's pruning, promising beautiful bouquets
    in spring
The Eve of March foretelling what secrets hidden beneath
the verdant soil soon to
    vitally burst into sight with hardy stalks with many
    hues of green
The immortal soul revels in Natures amazing silent force in
a mini cosmos into the
    immense macrocosmic, a declaration of the Divine
    Intelligence behind Creation.

The observer shifts in this reverie, thinking, drifting
thoughts by
        looking, truly seeing, absorbing natural beauty that
        binds all humanity
Misery can be decreased through conscious use of uniting
with this source
        that transcends fear, hatred, or
        attitudes that impoverish
It seems the world could use a new concept of that which
we call God,
        A new idea to be born in the minds and hearts of
        people everywhere
        of all possible positive belief systems
Expansion of amazing nature and each individualized
relationship
        to the Creator of all existence
Precious spirit available to all creating a direct experience
of one invisible
        yet truly known presence of pure untarnished Love.

GARDENING ANGEL

A garden is a place to witness the Divine
A garden is my place to unwind
Digging in the dirt with its marvelous smell
Seeing my flowers, knowing all so well

A bit of dirt, a clump of clay
From humble origins, great display
A refuge place for bird and human
Created by the gardener's skilled hand

A chunk of clay taken from bosom of earth
Worked and fashioned, artist's mirth
One day a vessel of noble grace
Fashioned by potter to just my taste

Graceful lines, perfect glaze
All from dirt, it does amaze
Humans have fashioned bits of clay
From earliest time for use and play
Tending the earth, it is such a prize
Skillful, acquiring knowing eyes

Earth is a living organism
Needing our loving care
Think of all it doth give
Beauty, bounty, our daily fare

Each fruit, vegetable, and slender reed
Has been provision for all we need
Sacred the earth on which we tread
Not to be despised and filled with lead

Sacred soil, gift from our Holy King
How could we pollute such a thing
Today begin afresh and new
To cherish the land given to you

Loving my tiny bit of soil
The hours here digging, are not toil
Planting the lovely ground
Giving thanks to Creator for sacred earth

AN IRIS IN BLOOM

There is an iris in bloom this morning
      speckled with droplets of gleaming water
It is mauve and cream standing like a queen
      surveying my garden green

Enjoying iris, so lovely, so fleeting
      waiting all year for their silent pageantry

Oh, Iris you are Queen of the garden
      even the regal rose
So willing and robust
      must take second place to you

You are the Queen
      the rose, the Royal Prince or Princess
Each magnificent but all must bow
      to the Queen Iris today

GLORIOUS GARDEN

Meditating upon a visual delight
    gracious rains at night
kissed by the Sun in the day
    causing the celebration
of new green garden growth
      exploding into sight

Strong stalks announcing
    future glories in the form
of flowers of many shapes
    colors vibrant and softly coy
having done their hidden alchemy
    beneath the soil

How can one small bulb
    produce such beauty?
Tiniest seeds sprout spurting
    surprising the aware eye
well-formed flowers of great vibrancy
      no painter can quite capture as well

A garden as a glorious gift
    but it takes a cooperative partnership
with the sun, rain, soil, and human hands
    tenderly tending, caring, feeding, pruning
encouraging each struggling plant
    and harnessing the unruly

Intruders are plucked and discouraged to go
  persistently, they seem to return
dormancy, like a deep winter's sleep
  is part of the rhythm of garden and gardener
a quiet more meditative time of introspection
    creating periods of vast productivity

ROSES AND ROTTERS

Dear Friends, and those whom I avoid —
In my garden faire
    this very early morning
Seeing your face
    praying your name

The variety of roses, brilliant orange calendulas
    and yellow, too
Purple lavender, coreopsis, Cecile Brunner
    geraniums, fuchsia, lobelia, succulents,
    which one are you?

And then the ones I do not like
    although it shames me so
I understood that garden faire
    has unwanted weeds, so in life
    I, too, attract my share

Thus, now when I see you,
    unfavored friend
Rather than dislike you so,
    I will remember,
in my soul scape
    you are a weed to know

Somehow, in this context
  I can find some peace
I laugh at
  my shallow dislikes
and rejoice in all I can release

Celebrating the many
  I love those whose
presence delights me
  and in this grace
I can bless them all
  and this day,
  my heart is free

WINTER, SPRING, SUMMER, FALL

Every life has a winter
    cold, deadening and bleak
The season of frozen in place
    afraid to think or speak

Then comes the thaw of a new idea
    the shift begins, the trickle, then flow
At last, winter is breaking up
    the idea or dream grows no matter how slow

Then the first shoots of spring
    new vitality begins to reign
The life has a lighter step and glow
    and soon one forgets winter's pain

Spring is all romance and roses
    perfume and fresh delight
Spring then romps into summer
    a time of long days, starry night

Summer is reaping the harvest fair
    flowers profuse, beauty all around
Summer is sweet fruit that drips from my mouth
    Summer is flow, treasure to be found

But in a while, the blossoms fade
    summer's hot sun begins to cool
A new season is lurking about
    I must not resist and play the fool

For summer cannot be my whole life
      for all sunshine would desert bring
Then, comes Fall with its dew and rain
      a time of subdued beauty, a brand-new thing

For in the fall comes Autumn fruit
      a bounty of a different kind
The leaves go scarlet, the breeze so cool
      A time of adventure, new paths to find

Fall is a time to pick and gather
      Knowing that winter will surely come
The storage of goods and planning ahead
      Soon bare trees, say fall is done

A time of hibernation, repose, asleep
      The earth rejuvenates in quiet rest
Now incubating new dreams and goals
      An awakening, we rejoice, each season is blessed

LAVENDER

The lavender
salutes the Sun.
Every stem bends
in humble homage.
The sweet aroma and
purple bloom
speaks a truth louder
than any sage.

"Go to the light,
find energy fine.
Go to the light,
a touch of the Divine."

"Go to the light,
open heart and head.
Go to the light
and be deeply fed."

SPIRAL OF LIFE

The yellow blossoms of neighbor's large tree drift like
graceful wee fairies to the ground
Rocks tumble being disrupted by roof, foot, or natures
erosion, sliding, rolling to the ground
Rose petals all bloomed out float silently upon the soft
breeze to the awaiting ground
Giant mother trees, many hundreds of years old eventually
begin to weaken, thus the dying process until one day they
fall shattering upon the forest floor

Not being mindful, stretching with one leg upon my
kitchen counter
my balance lost crashing to the hard floor
precursor perhaps how we all in that allowed appointment
with departure, shall in casket
or as ash to be carefully placed into the ground
So, it seems is the circle of life, the ground receives with
ample embrace using each fallen thing to become mulch or
microbes for the next cycle appearing, disappearing

All comes from the earth—food to nourish, water to
hydrate, minerals, growth of every imaginable type, size,
shape, fragrance, and use
We ourselves are made of the same elemental components—
earth, air, water, fire, minerals and the ethers

All life exchanges its energetic vitality back into the
mother's bosom to change form
and be born again into a new imaginative energetic
expression
The spiral of life ascending, descending constantly forever
Even the star's dust is a living part of humanity; nothing
is totally separate,
all fused together on the great play of cosmic life upon itself
out of itself into itself, again and again, in eternity's spiral
of Creation

MEDITATIVE TIME IN THE GARDEN

Joy! Sun this morning so bright it startles my eyes
     after many consecutive days of welcome rain
a few cuttings and wildflower seeds carefully placed in
     wet, soggy earth awaiting new members of our
     green family.

The warmth on face, head, back feels glorious
     energizing Sun call me outside, no longer house bound.
A siren calls for sun worshipping California woman loving
her garden
     clipping, cleaning, bringing order to small busy
     crowded plot of earth
     as well as patios, decks long neglected from
     profuse rainfall.

Much to care for, but a work that feeds something deep
within me,
     fingers in the earth have long been a centering practice.
Enjoying moist receiving soil so willing to feed and support
the new
     seeds awaiting roots, shoots, and eventually blooms
     of varying kinds.

A time of waiting, watching, looking forward to Mother
Nature's bounty
      come spring.
Now a time of preparation leading to a season of
celebration, riots of colors
      shapes, scents and secrets revealed ... ahh ... spring.

Bulbs placed in the dark loam yet forgotten, a queen gowned
in purple like
      royalty.
Of all my spring appearances, iris takes front stage display,
glorious and regal in
      her presence standing upright, goddess-like, so stately.

Then the daffodils, freesias, ranunculus, and a few shy tulips —
      each a beauty in their own way, the colors unique to
      each varietal.
I could not live joyously without green and growing things
about me
      like friends, sharing my sacred sanctuary space.

Each has been invited, meticulously cared for then comes
the reward —
      joy on a stem!
Perfumed in a graceful blossom, beauty that delights the
eyes and gives a sweet
      blessing to the soul.

Soul food for the darker times eclipsed by spring and
summer when the fruit tree's
> lusciousness, burdened with the round, splendor from
> my spreading plum tree.

Delicious golden orbs appear upon majesty apricot, the royal
delight of
> friends, family, neighbors, busy birds, ravenous
> raccoons, and all walkers
> passing by, and me.

Kumquats small, orange, sweet sourness flavoring many a dish
> abundant enough to share and spare.

Meyer lemons faithful in its seemingly perfectly shaped
citrus fruit for summer
> and fall and, oh, the compact sweetness of Anna apples
> rounding out the bountiful summer fare.

Mother Nature and I dance together in harmonious
enjoyment of the co-creative
> cooperative effort, like spirits intertwined in the oldest
> of artistic, practical pursuits.

In great gratitude reflecting that it is lovely to enjoy this
sunny cool winter day in
> quiet solitary walking meditation, aware of the great
> goodness of being a part of this life.

GARDEN PRAYER

Oh joy, a morning in the garden
A few hours in the sunlight
The song of the birds, the flowers in bloom
Making my heart-mind bright

Thank You for the wisdom in creation
Of the life force that livens all about me
The radiance of spring slipping quickly into summer
A visual feast expressing divine vibrancy

Praise Be!

THE LEAF

Autumn leaf fallen on street black
A part of God's Creation, some of the All
What intelligence forged this leaf,
With veins, design, and colors of fall

This leaf was a bud upon a branch
Life expressing itself in force
It grew day-by-day from smallest start
Into regal grand attached until divorce

Then it fell from high above
And tumbled to the ground
My morning walk and reading time
This leaf called me round

I stooped and picked leaf up
Examining rare beauty there
Why a leaf? What purpose formed
For me to pluck and stare?

It grew to serve in many ways
Shelter for the bug and bird
And shade on long, hot sunny days
Music rustling at evening heard

In spring, all tender and green
Summer in full array
Then comes fall, its colors turn
Separating from tree, down and away

But upon the ground, it still gives life
To waiting earth beneath
A slow decay to humus soil
Enriching seedlings, its life bequeath

A spiritual trust is playing out here
A message from the Divine
Every phase of life has its good
For eternity is in every time

The energy flows from root to limb
New leaves are budding more
The nutrients that come from soil
from leaves that came before

HOW FAIRE THE MORNING

How faire the morning
    crisp and cold
So bright the Sun
    sky stunning bold
The rain kissing the earth
    with life-giving force
All through the night
    now a lull no remorse

Celebrate a rain-washed day
    all sparkly and alive
Every leaf on every plant
    glistens like a prize

Feeling renewal each morning
    what has gone before is past
This day is fresh and new
    partaking a welcome repass

Gratitude for a sunny morning
    shining like a jewel
Sighting new plants popping through
    soil replenished by life's renewal

May I hold each morning
    wet, sunny or gray
As a gift received from giver great
    celebrating being alive today

PROMISES FROM THE GARDEN

An old hymn goes and dances through my head,
"I come to the garden to pray, while the dew is still in
the meadow"

Gardening is a joy
the angels play with me there
In each bright face of flower fine
I see a hint of the Great Divine

Holy work is here to view
Blessed handiwork you do
From plainest seed comes bloom so bright
Assuring me that things are right

One cannot fear in garden work
Occupying both mind and hand
Dark shadows that at night may lurk
In morning sun, joy walks the land

The promise of a fresh new day
Is rich in all that life may play
A win, a windfall, a miracle will come
Just be aware of each bright crumb

Here a smile, there a hug
A penny found, a coffee mug
A letter from a friend away
The loving words to you they say

"You're special"
"We love you"
"You're our choice"
In all these gifts, I hear God's voice

Miracles, yes are everywhere
This day, a golden garment wear
Walk like a goddess upon the earth
Be like a queen given re-birth
In your heart, majestic be
And fruits of love, your harvest see

Uplift your world with noble stance
Lighten hearts with kindly glance
Be a queen in your garden land
Here goodness, kindness, may always stand

SUNDAY MORNING – SILENT SACRAMENT

Behind the Great Ones stand
ever awaiting bidding come forth
out of darkness all things appear
all that is born comes into form
        from the Unseen

The seed harbors the thing
that is to be—tree or flower
years it can wait before
a cracking shaft of light
            enters the Unseen

The womb hidden away in body darkness
awaiting sperms invading arrival
months of undisclosed formation
body, hands, limbs, brain appear
            to birth the Unseen

Empathy, compassion ferment in pain
heartbreak, illness, or lonely dark hours
purification burning away of ego's dross
creating its own alchemical magic
            before Unseen is seen

Solace for the soul is the knowledge
that all of life spawns from unawaken
dark nights of painful sojourn
holy crucible conceiving new life
            Blessed Unseen

chapter 3

Listening Is a Silent Force

A SILENT FORCE

In the beauty of this moment
tranquil flowers, songbirds
    a joyous, background serenade
Warmth of the faithful radiant sun
    awakening a springing forth of this
    most magical season
Spring is bursting into a beauteous
    display of new offerings of lemons with roses
    foliage, flowers, other luscious fruits

A pondering question often asked
    "How many hues of green
    from vivid to subdued?"
Displaying all on the color wheel spectrum
    bold and pastels, mixtures of several
    sometimes captured in one leaf
Roses robust in their first flashy showing
    an energetic salute to spring after a
    long slumbering, sap low, resting winter

Showy like a teenaged girl quivering with excitement
    adorned with radiant aliveness
    so is nature's first rapturous blush
The magnificent blue above gentle as an intimate embrace
    and this morning absent of any wispy clouds
    glorious life broadcasting encouragement generously
Beauty is tangible like appreciation from our hearts
    each vibration of adoration for the infinite life force
    creating, maintaining every possible living expression

This new day announcing rebirth, belonging within this
silent force
      sending blessings from the treasure chest of my heart to
      all life, each and every living thing on our lovely planet
May the reality of this force of love sending positive
vibrational
      energies be well received, just as the Sun illuminates
      each surface of growth vitalizing and touching
Listening is a silent force
      available to all, a blessing today and evermore!

TO WHOM I SPEAKE

Not knowing to whom i speak
    or whose response speaking within me
        into the spaciousness created by silence

There is that great unknown
    and yet knowable presence coming forth
        faithful as one's next breath

Sometimes the voice is esoteric, ephemeral
    others practical, directive
        or chatty, cute even humorous

Some mornings it is lyrical, poetic,
    but most cherished is the deep wisdom coming
        from a knowledge beyond myself

Occasionally aware when sound asleep I am pulled away
from earth's
    psychic pull of collective consciousness, lifted
    to a realm
        for which I have no name or description

What I garner is a sense of being instructed, taught things
    where in the earth realm, this has not been
    my privilege
        to be formally educated in a noteworthy
        university

The knowing that appears at times upon the page
    is a combination of my earth walk, reading, learning,
        working, joined with a silent spacious
        communication

This has expanded my understanding of higher
    deeper expressions responsive words upon a page is
        "we" and this somehow is comfortable to me

A collection of ascended souls, angelics or
    wise ones, ancestral guides
        seem just right

From earliest childhood being drawn to pictures of angels
    not questioning why in my childish mind
        just intuitively enjoyed seeing these
        etheric beings

Growing into early school years living with a small
group of nuns
    being introduced to Bible stories, often
    referring to angels
        a context of identification was formed

Also, stories of saints, prophets, and ancestral figures
    thus, a group of guardians did not seem unnatural
        to my young growing inner framework

Here I sit this rainy morning being prompted somehow
      to scribble these musing upon empty notebook page
            freely flowing as natural as breathing

It must be my soul journey for this latter season of my life
      never having a sense of being alone or ceasing to be
            amazed at what flows forth from
            hand-written words

A persistent inner urging to share with others what has
graciously
      been gifted to me fills my heart with
      overwhelming gratitude
            for the spaciousness of silence not meant
            for me alone

THE JOURNEY TO STILLNESS

First, I become quiet
    turning off all exterior noise
        within and without

The quiet of muscles, sinew, and mind
    my inner self still searches
        for a distraction

Yet I wait and soon it calms
    quiet, relaxing
        deep rhythmic breathing
Then the stillness
    the blessed
        sacred stillness

STILLNESS

Stillness is where the
    crystals are formed
Stillness is where a
    diamond receives its
      brilliance

Stillness is where
    the waters run deep
Stillness is in being,
    not performing

Stillness is where
    a heart
begins to beat in
    lovely union
with the rhythm
    written by the Divine's heart

Stillness is where
    the light
so incredibly lovely
    and translucent
illuminates the soul
    of those
      finding this delight

Stillness is always here
  Why would I avoid this life?
Stillness awaits those who
  will come
It has always been
  ever available
   deep within our inner light

Still, stilled, stillness —

LISTENING IS HOLY AND SACRED

So glorious the day! Speake to me a prayerful request
the speaking is in the air, the constant gift of breath
the message is in the beauty of life everywhere apparent
the musical song of the day is the rustling of leaves ruffled
by the
     breeze, and cheery chirping of our feathered friends

The blue above writes large cosmic love letters of abundance
where there is companionship of air, water, earth and fire
the very elements of all beings, and within our bodies
the lungs oxygenating the entire structure with each intake
     exhaling, releasing the processed breath

Water running constantly throughout the veins, organs, and
giving forth
the metabolized fluids back to earth
minerals build our bones, teeth, hair
strengthening muscular system
     each mineral doing a heroic function

Fire warms our blood, passion in the belly
heart and mind's energy firing from the elemental force
needed to be kept in balance,
each elemental particle has a voice
     and is speaking; listen

Listening is key to being spoken to
the more receptive the listener within,
the more vital the voice
the listener is the Holy One within
receptive, responsive and inspirer of the finer way to walk
        upon this beautiful earth

Cherishing all of nature's sensing,
dancing concerto of joyous greeting
to each new dawning
        a never-before birthed day
sacred, holy as we deeply listen

"The blessings of the Infinite are fresh and new every morning."
Rejoice!

DIVINE EXPRESSION OF THE ONE

Thoughts from infinity arrive on angels' wings
      whispering the living word into the listening ear
Courageous actions aided by Archangels mighty power
      Inspirational words flowing from the river of
      revelation
      whispered by the ancient masters
Musical melodies, songs sung from the ethers by
      many heavenly voices

Great works, feats of engineering, inventions emanating
      powerfully, purposefully from the collective wise ones
Loving acceptance, compassion, acts of kindness encouraged
      by golden stream of sweetness from our ancient
      ancestors
Tolerance and forgiveness encouraging us by the soundless
      Substance of life impressed by untold ascended souls

Beautiful, loving care of Mother Earth championed by
      her creative principle of lavish generosity
Tilling the ground bringing forth fruit and flowers,
a diving circuit
      of loving impulses by nature's guardians
      the divas, elementals, also nature sprites

Babies are birthed gifted with angelic guardians,
      lifelong companions shepherding them through
      childhood and each day of their lives

Small innocent children are often aware of these unseen
friends as an essence of love surrounding them

We are all surrounded by such a great crowd of witnesses
Each living thing is a designated divine expression
        of the One Infinite Love
Call upon any holy name and the universal presence
        always and ever available

The Great Teacher called upon the Father as a clarity
        for mostly an unlearned populace,
        few with privilege of formal education
Father, a most intimate utterance for a small child
        designating sonship, offspring, bloodlines, family

Thus, all are of the Father Creator, Divine Intelligence
        Infinite Love flowing to all Creation
In truth, we are interrelated with each other,
        making us one people, brothers, sisters
        a human family around the entire planet

All the unseen presences are available to us
        whispering this truth into our heart-minds
        again and again,
"We are one; we are all one with the One and Only One
        There is no other!"

BIRDS SINGING COSMOS RINGING

The solemn fog silently creeps onto the land of our
beachfront town
draped with gray mist, and yet the birds sing!
They must be our morning teacher of celebration, exalting
life no matter how it looks.

Oh birds, so small and fair
I hear you singing there
What joy bubbles through tiny frame?
What fire ignites your joyous flame?

Share with me your secret, dear
Share the triumphant spirit here
In your wee presence is music and mirth
Send your songs into my heart to birth

The excitement, the joy, the jubilee
Can you not share this miracle with me?
Perhaps the secret is in the singing
So to this day, my voice I'm bringing
Sing a song to celebrate love
Love for all, below and above

Joy for legs that take me far
Praise for dreams upon one star
Yes, the secret is in the singing
Sing a song through the Cosmos ringing

CHAMBER OF SILENCE

In this moment, stepping into that chamber of silence,
listening
Desiring your presence, companionship, and voice
Come Lord of all; speak your eternal wisdom.
The Chamber of Silence is our own special place to retreat

We know it well. We are here, as always. As near as your
request, your next breath.
There is not a molecule on the planet where we are
not present.
There is a collective Omnipotence, many expressions,
multiple voices, yet
all speaking the same Song of Oneness.

These may be guides, angels, ascended masters, all souls on
their journeys,
but still individualizations of the One who is loving, serving
through the expression of the infinite enlightened nature
In truth there can be no separation, only within one's
thinking or individual's choice.

Any breath can be the breath that breathes a prayer,
and the Holy One
ever conscious awareness of each soul calling.
So, beloved, always call.
There will always be an answer.

Sometimes the answer is silent, but potent with presence.
Sometimes the answer is too much to say conveying a new precept or concept.
Sometimes the answer is just an emanation of pure love filling your empty-feeling places.
Sometimes an idea, a next indicated step, or action or nonaction to take.
Sometimes is just "Hello, beloved" and blessing you on your way for the day.

Soul guides are always available; knock and the door will open. Call, the answer shall come.
Empathy and comfort beyond the physical senses shall descend upon you.
Question and the inner probing will be profound.
Yes, beloved, We are always here. The Great Divine in you is what you may call We.

The infinite is ever listening, the only one who
Moves, breathes, lives as a presence of creative energy.
As a fish in water providing its every need — air, food, climate, fellow fish,
hiding places, sunlight, variety of life experience.

As it is with you and all living things.
We live, move, breathe, have our being in the omnipresent substance
that sustains, maintains, and mentors everything that exists.
There can be no separation, ever.

THREE STEPS FORWARD

Stepping stones are a means of crossing a pond or river,
perhaps a muddy patch taking one forward to a desired
location or destination
anticipating filling a long felt interior void
    Many, a question and uncertainty arise to be
    examined, embraced
    or eliminated to step into an awaiting possibility
    these three steps take many forms throughout
    a human's soul journey

The idea is the first stepping stone—birthing
birthing of a conscious decision, inner prompting,
or following a dream
Birthing is not always an easy process
    a period of forming the egg into embryo
    a child to be, a new invention in the physical or oneself
    an awkwardness, ungainly time of uncertainty, doubts,
    and anticipation

Maintaining is the second stone forward
maintaining the original resolve with supportive nutrients,
physically
or mental, spiritual reinforcement through numerous means
    Determination and inner integrity are a component
    of this step
    a promise to self to follow through is sacred and not
    to be broken
    just as our word is our bond to be impeccable in our
    personal orbit

The last stepping stone is *dissolving*
strange that once a project, dream, invention, book, or child
has been birthed,
it takes on a life, a persona of its own in the public domain
> There is joy at having completed the steps, crossing
> a rushing river or
> treacherous terrain causing great personal learning
> and expansion
> of the inner and outer circumstances than the one
> taking last steps

Like a timid foot onto the very first exploratory step
forward, a restructured shift
finding betterment in everything, a broader and deeper
experience,
> a higher realization
> a greater good
> stepping forward onto each chosen stone

OUR CREATOR GIVES UNCEASINGLY

See the sunlight pierce the darkness
Radiant beams of early morning light
Shoot like fingers into the darkness
Then as a child fingerpaints, spreading with delight

See the flower bud and bloom
The glorious miracle of opening
The color, the shape, perfume, and grace
The dying back bringing forth seeds popping

 See the rain that comes from where,
A few scattered clouds, then more
The waters from heaven that nourish the earth
Bringing refreshment, new life to my door

Seeing the seasons come and go
Spring, summer, winter, and fall
Each has a magic, a beauty rare
Increasing creativity from the mother of all

The rain falls on the just and the unjust
The loving divine is for one and all
Forgiveness is seeing with Christ eyes
Rain is impartial, we too, can answer this call

Our Creator gives unceasingly
Love, beauty, joy, and peace
Entering into a larger place
Familiar narrow thinking release

SEASONAL GIFTS

August, so soon, how the days go ...

First it was April, spring's all aglow
Then it was June without its gloom
Then came July, stars and stripes fly
Summer upon us with long hot days
Beach time and BBQ, early morn haze
Now comes hot August, summer full blast
A short time of heat that we know will not last

Then comes September, a month most glorious
Beautiful days, long lovely nights
Indian summers for which we're notorious
Then winter, slower, colder
some plants and mammals hibernating
A time of silent, solitary reflection

Seasons come and seasons go
Consistent is the mother, this I know!

AH, MUSINGS

oh, hear the song of the birds
bursting with the joy of life today
how contagious their song
my heart mind opens to embrace
receive the joy of the gift life is
receive the lightness of song
receive the celebration of a new day
receive what was mine
                    all along

SO GLORIOUS THE DAY

So Glorious the day, speaking to me a prayerful request
the speaking is in the air, the constant gift of breath
the message is in the beauty of life everywhere apparent
the musical song of the day is the sound of rustling leaves
ruffled by the breeze, and cheery chirping of
our feathered friends

The blue above writes large cosmic love letters of abundance
ever there is companionship, of air, water, earth, and fire
the very elements of all living beings; and within our bodies,
the lungs oxygenating the entire structure with each intake
then exhaling the processed breath

Water running constantly throughout the veins,
organs and giving forth the metabolized fluids back to earth
minerals build our bones, teeth, hair,
strengthening muscular system
each mineral doing a heroic function

Fire warms our blood, passion in the belly
heart and mind's energy firing from this elemental force
needing to be kept in enriched balance
each elemental partial has a voice and is speaking,
quietly listen!

Listening is key to being spoken to
the more receptive the listener within, the more vital
the voice
the listener is the holy one within, a receptive, responsive
and inspirer of the finer way to walk
upon this beautiful Planet Earth

Cherishing all of nature's sensing
dancing concerto of joyous greeting
for each morning dawning new,
a never-before birth to be cherished day.

"The blessings of the Infinite are fresh and new every morning."

SOLITUDE DELIGHTS

The chimes dance to a
lively song
composed by summer
breezes
    Delights

Laguna's flag
faded fair
ripples in the
gentle air
unfurled, open
then curled fully
    Delights

A gentle day of
slower pace
movements more
measured
awaiting a shift
into recognition
    Delights

The air stops
still
silence blankets
the scene
quiet so soft
embracing
a far-off hum
ah, quiet
    Delights

TWO TREES

Two trees planted side-by-side
       same nutrients placed around root ball
           weather conditions, environment, origin,
       same gardener
           all caring for them equally

The trees sat in thought feeling the new space,
       their lifelines were placed into the dark,
           unfamiliar, long silent trepidation
           exploring the unknown

One tree after sitting in the silence
       a long, lonely time, searching for what was liked
           felt courage to send a few roots deeper
           into dark unknown

The further those first inquiries reached
       a surrendering into the unfamiliar
           finding surprisingly welcomed
           by unknown

In time, sustenance encouraged growth,
       more root tendrils ventured further,
           wider; the circle of existence became
           no longer unknown

The other tree thought fearfully,
  afraid of this new place crying "why me"
    frightened to delve into generous Mother Earth
   resisting the unknown

This tree paled and shriveled beside
  the blossoming other, same elements,
    one lived expanding, the other resisting
   alienated by the unknown

chapter 4

Earth's Bountiful Gifts

THE ANCIENT, ANCIENT

Rocks, I love rocks
    warm flat rocks
    heated by Brother Sun
    who knows them well

Rocks that have stood throughout the ages
    rain, sun, flood, and drought
    have pummeled
    these monument formations

For out of the fires of Earth's upheaval,
    they were formed and cast forth
    to adorn our world, Ancestors knew well

Speak your wisdom that we may hear
    upon your surface, placing an ear
    hearing the gnashing of first Creation
    feeling ancient music's wild sensation

You seem solid, a gift of being alive
    energy within you moves like a hive
    molecules bouncing, sending forth a word
    every once in a while, you are quietly heard

Now is a time, O Ancient Wonder
    that we open our receptors down under
    and hear at a level beyond mere sound
    and in the hearing, may wisdom be found

I have embraced you in far off land
    hugged you as grains of sand
    kissed you as crystals rare
    as a fossil lovely, now I wear

O Ancient of Ancients, the mud, the clay
    taking in my hand and begin to play
    shaping you into vessel fair
    for worship, fashioning you there

Dirt is the holiest of gems
    from which all life does flow
    oil, food, trees, water, and raw cloth
    from Thee, O Sacred Earth below

You are the Ancient that hides the old
    in your bosom, secrets you hold
    all comes from you, all will return
    celebrate Ancient Earth, from whom we learn

CELEBRATION OF THE GIFTS GIVEN

I celebrate this day, the gifts given
Sight to see the glory of spring
Hearing which revels in the song of birds
The sweet scent of morning air, moist and perfumed
The feel of earth beneath my feet,
my sweet perfect feet that trod my path so well

My legs, so faithful to carry me far
My back straight and strong
My lungs, stomach, bowels and teeth, my inner workings
profound
My hands, my tools to do and bless, to touch and heal
My hair, my eyelashes, my altogether wonderful body

How to praise such wisdom creating all, fully equipped for
life and godliness
Choosing who we will serve, infinity or worldly materialism,
Our inner voice or outer cry
Sentenced by only that which we accept as all our shackles
We do in this moment now, release all that no longer serves
A releasing, letting go, celebrating freedom and this precious
gift of choice

Opening ourselves to the fresh, the new, the vital
    Now alive as we have never been before
        Free, free, free to be
           The best we can be
             Spirit in all
               As each
               Through each
               So it shall be!

THE GIFT

We now accept the gift of time
Given me by a loving hand, so kind
Time to stand quietly at window
Watching the birds in garden aglow

A pair of robins in birdbath there
Frolicking and bathing, a splendid affair
He with Christmas red upon his breast
She with dullest brown understated dress

He with crimson head, a beacon bright
Attracting all within a garden's sight
She, all colors subdued, in splashing bath
While he on guard watches with a laugh

How clever of nature to make him so
The object of attention protects, you know
The female not so interestingly adorned
Is by predator, missed or scorned

But he in his masculine way
With colors flashing, saves the day
Quick to alert his Lady Gray
Shows his love with sassy say

A gift given in quiet time
To observe the marvel around
Robin Red Breast and Lady Dull Breast
Delighting my soul and tickling the mind

HARMONY

Stay with harmony inside and out
Dance with harmony all through the day
Melding all thoughts, feelings, responses
Orchestration a divine melody

Empty places now filling
wounded spaces releasing
Harmonizing the whole being
A loving breath, each inhale, then exhale

Each breathe adds and subtracts
Dropping the surplus
Adding only pure golden realities
Harmony has no discordant notes

May each individual instrument
Bring forth the melodious sound
Enriching the entire piece
Of unified masterful music

Allow the great genius of all motions
To come forth as the harmonious
Individualized Maestro
Uniquely expressed and enjoyed

Lovingly shaped to be just the right melody
Producing music out into the universal symphony
Be a song sound of delight this day, singing
"May all the world be blessed" a prayer song
        reverberating throughout the Earth

LOVE'S REDEMPTION

Redemption, paid debt, off the hook
What a gift, what a thing to receive
What have we done to deserve such love?
All unfolded, none to leave

None to leave to the hell of their own making
You are simply and beautifully being, you
Love loves and knows only to Love
Love does not have to forgive, no pardon due

For love sees the object of its love in perfection
As a parent sees an unskillful child learning to walk
Falling and perhaps breaking a lamp or vase
No recrimination to wee child, just kind, gentle talk

The parent sees their child as a delight
Understanding the difficulty in learning to live
Nurtures, guides, guards and endeavors to direct
This is love, the eternal heart existing to give

So our redemption canceled shortages
Are not because of us or our doing
But because you are expressing that which you are —
Love, pure, exquisite, joyous redemption.

INSTIGATOR OF INSPIRATION

You are the Divine living, loving presence
    resident within us all
You are the instigator of inspiration
    the strength of positive purpose
The sustainer of the life force
    within us all

You are the healer, encourager, mentor, teacher
    infinite wisdom eternal
You are the loving impulse within the hearts and minds
    of all who turn in thousands of differing ways to you
Calling in many diverse expressions, yet all are heard
    seen, acknowledged

Intimately known down to the very hairs upon each head
    filling open minds, hearts and speech
With wisdom and expanded sight and understanding
    of the higher concepts of creation
Great gratitude for holding our hands and guiding
each hesitant
    step on this, our Earth Walk journey

May your words flow in, through and as our deepest
    inner thoughts, attitudes, and action
A warm presence of cherishing ever present companion
    pure love, joy, peace, and harmony
Resident in every part of all willing beings, then reflected out
    to an awakening, healing world

BUTTERFLY GIFT

If a butterfly lands upon your hand
and sits poised with glorious open wings
coming out of the frenetic energy of life,
revere that moment, for there, Creation sings.

If a butterfly finds you among all the rest
and gently pauses upon your open hand,
rejoice that you have been touched,
together commune slowly entering love's land.

Oh, dear ones blessed by fortune
to have love's emissary enter your world,
if this butterfly lands in your hand,
don't squeeze, crushing love's wings unfurled.

MY GIFT — THE ANGELS OF TIME

You see me as ugly little black specks,
Nothing of truth and beauty here
Yet within is a shining stranger
Waiting to give a gift to you dear

Place me in a favorite spot
Give me sun and soil fine
Water me and in the turning time
You will clearly see me shine

For I will, in a moment of magic
Rise from the silent dark
Into the light, giving shape to matter
The angel of time now embarks

This little seed, so plain and willing
Is a condensed collection of energy divine,
A light beam of love contained
It's soul parent births this gift of a magic time

SEASONS

Loving the touch of tough, leathery leaves
    with dainty orchid flowers
There is such strength in this plant
    it seems to grow in a matter of hours

The life force in my garden
    is my constant delight
The springing forth of new growth
    popping from brown earth into my sight

Harvesting sweet pea seeds
    early this Sunday morn
The promise of future beauty
    in little round black seeds born

The cycle of life all about me
    birth, growth, blossoming and dying
A message repeated, again and again
    a dance danced without any trying

Being only an observer
    of the magnificent mysteries
But in the observation
    learning our own intricacies

Do we not conceive an idea or dream
    birthed, nurtured, blossom and die?
The cycles within our own lives
    seasons upon which one may rely

BULBS MEDITATION

The earth is cold and damp
    yet the Divine Mother of all
        goes into the earth to meditate
            three days, three nights
                exchanging energies

She arises stronger having gained the earth's energy
    the earth is revitalized by her divine presence
        reciprocity is the law of the universe
            one must give to receive—sharing is caring
                exchanging life force

Having gone deep within the cold dampness
    the interior landscape desiring exchange of energies
        intend to release the past and leave behind
        non-serving
            and accepting silent powerful preparation
            for newness
                forgive, release, open to vital true
                soulfulness

Radically pruning garden roses of dead wood toxic
old growth
    metaphorically my inner journey in outer expression
        thinking towards the spring of new growth
    and beauty
            the interior landscape understands this
            quiet time
                of healing, meditation, prayer
                and writing

A gift of tulips brings new thoughts to this life-
enriching process
in faith one places a dry bulb into the awaiting
sleeping earth
unseen forces work all winter enriching
and energizing
until that seemingly magic moment when
a stalk
bursts from the ground testifying
to life force

So it is with the human seeking newness into one's true
soul purpose
tilling the soil of inner being, a discarding, enriching,
prayerfully
a slow process to tending, caring, disciplined
dedication
just as the garden responds so do we
metaphysically
the law of cause and effect always
at work

The seed planted, tended, nourished, allowed water and light
will surely sprout into that which was the original
purpose
a seed of intention is as potent, powerful
and sure
choose carefully what you desire to see
in life
it will reap in future bringing newness
to the soul

STONES

Stones, stones, ancient stones
I have sought you around the world
Since childhood, these earthly treasures
Have called to me with a voice felt, not heard

Some stones, I could pluck from old ground
Others, I could just gaze and place my palms
Against your antique, hand-carved strength
Still standing solid testaments to long days

Stonehenge was a forbidden monument for touch
But a very old elder welcomed my inquiring fingers
In Avery resting my air flight infected eyes
Against the cold stone asking for healing, silently

An old crone, was she real or an apparition?
Appeared from where I know not, but there she was
"Ahhh, they are still alive," she spoke in country English
"But those awoke first," pointing to stones standing
Across the road like mighty sentinels awaiting what?

When I looked back, she was gone; where so quickly?
Crossing the country road to commune with silent
monuments
Enjoying touching, sensing what I could, unaccustomed to such
The drizzle increased and wind began, so I sought cover

In a small pub nearby, entering to see a joyous crowd
by the fire
All dressed in Green Man outfits celebrating,
I believe, Beltane
They had been doing ceremony at some mystical site,
seeking now the pub
We talked, laughed, and I thought, these are the
Living Stones,
gifts I can understand.

I KNOW SPRING IS HERE

Picking my first brodiaea today
    knowing that spring is here
        not by the passage of time
            or calendar date proclaiming blossom dear

But I know because I saw the earth
    presenting me with a gift from the bosom of itself
        small purple puff on slender stalk
            yet one of my very favorites in blue delft

I, like most love spring and its gifts
    so varied in shape and hue
        spring is a time when in deep thought
            I remember the essence of you

The earth gave me a sweet gift
    created in love for all including me
        my hand so grateful plucked
            just one to take home to see

As always, gratitude fills my heart
    with the bounty of blessing so wide
        but it takes observing and remembering
            to listen to the sweet voice inside

I was given a brodiaea today
    I carry my prize gently homeward
        knowing that spring surely has come
            beauty in my heart, a living word

TOUCH STONES

Art, mementos, things I like
Put everywhere within my sight
Each awakens a memory or dream
Others excite imagination to scheme

No wonder I have so many things
For from each gift or item, memory springs
These are my touch stones to other places
Each has attached diverse lovely faces

The places I have gathered a memento or two
From rocks, seashells, artworks, not a few
Street art graces my office wall
Taking me back to visit them all

Even my closet is a treasure trove
Shirts, sweaters, items worn as I rove
My travels are dear, rich with delight
How can I banish my gatherings from sight?

Well, am I the clutter queen?
Gathering, picking, collecting at every scene
Enjoying things; they are my own delight
Exciting my inner world keeping all in my sight

THE GIFT OF RAIN

Gratefully loving the rain, living in
    drier Southern California
The gentle spring rain that kisses
    flower and fauna with softest touch

The driving rains of winter are welcome
    after the sizzling glare of summer
The dew, the rain, the moisture
    Bringing so much to my world

Having seen the storm of rapid
    fire sparks that pelt the skin
And rain so kind, that one in joy stands
    with open mouth receiving

Rains so cold that frozen pellets
    bombard friend and foe
For the rain, the blessed rain
    falls on the just and the deceiving

Rain is our lifeline from Heaven
    bringing needed moisture
Rain is the definition of seasons
    with watery song

Do you not hear the music tapping
    on skylight or windowpane?
A dance of joyous life nourishing
    the waiting earth, and souls thirsty so long

Oh, then the miracle gift arrives
    a multicolored statement across the sky
Rainbow, rainbow, full of hope and beauty
    Eternal promise is proof we do not die

CIRCULATING ENERGIES

Circles of life, the circulating energies upon and
    through the planet
ever moving circulating with fresh currents like a vortex's
spiraling in the eternal spiral
whirling with energy animating airstreams feeding
the atmosphere

Round and round tighter and tighter the movement go,
then like dancing waters in a spa whirlpool, foam and ripples out
into the whole body of awaiting waters
    Is this not like humanity's existence upon this lovely
    green blue multi-colored planet?

Human DNA circulating from the human vortex of
    male semen into the fertile seed
hidden cherished sacred bowl of the female creating new
fertile life, again and again
    The cross pollination of humanity has seeded
    and reseeded the growing tribes
and nomadic wanderers until all are presently known;
humanity is carrying the same basic DNA

One humanity, one people with individualized
    sequencing making the beautiful blend of
skin in many hues, sizes, elegant eyes in myriad of shades,
variations of hair texture
coloration, unique features each stature and build, yet all
one people
created from the One Eternal Source of all Creation

Numerous beliefs, customs, traditions, foods, clothing,
    songs and dances,
an array of languages, variously named countries
and territories,
an unlimited variety of fascinating expressions of the Divine
in human form
    Same specular scenario in the animal kingdom, plant
    world, minerals,
and all forms of living things

    Expanding, morphing, changing over eons of time;
    centuries circulating the wide
expression of ever evolving life into various, subtle,
dramatic and occasionally
spectacular progressions of abilities, appearances and
consciousness

    How marvelous all one as untold miracles of life by the
    universal rhythm of spiritual
unfolding like fresh water flowing, bubbling, animating each
by its energetic presence
    Most amazing the circulating gift of life generously
    given, each and every day,
breath by breath, like drops of energizing rain falling
where it will

ABUNDANT SUBSTANCE

The sweet beauty of a pansy flower face
The energy of birds at the feeder
Excitement of a kitten
This energetic urge of life to express itself from itself
into itself

Life's replication in every conceivable imaginable form
from stars to starfish, ants to antelopes
earthworms to elephants
all possessing the same energetic substance from source

A champion runner and a toddler learning to walk
The wonder of the invisible bounty of unceasing force
of pure love
Activation equated into movement,
producing massive achievements

Basking in the basic chain of life through a pure
profound genius
This pipeline of joyous abundant substance is for everyone
Every created thing has accessibility, yet not all
avail themselves
Cosmic resources await being tapped, channeled, displayed
by simple steps
As well as major human jumps, shifts of seemingly
miraculous movement

At Creation's dawning process, every needed component
came forth
From which an unending substance began and continues
to evolve
How marvelous the wonder of this ongoing eternally
erupting
Perfection-play of life of which all are participants partaking
marvelously

Abundant enriching wonder, thrusting us towards
An evolutional unfolding of the harmonious template
Originated through the Divine Intelligence of magical
proportions
Moving Creation ever forward

LIQUID CRYSTALS

Droplets of dew
    rainbow splatters
        reflections of the moon upon a mud puddle
           a refreshing sip
               a warm relaxing shower
                   swimming caressed and held
The life-giving substance for all living things —
    water, the elixir of the Universe and all dwelling
    thereon
        eyes of every species gazing in wonder
        and delight
           at a lake, stream, river, pond, sea or awe-
           inspiring ocean
               desiring to touch, drink, immerse,
               perhaps ride upon
                   flowing tides, rapids, waterfalls
Sounds of moving waters awakening the senses
    Is it evoking ancient memories
        perhaps of living in the sea?
           Crawling, hesitating, scratching onto
           terra firma,
               resting nibbling exploring with sight,
               all sensations
                   now uncomfortable retreating
                   to liquid home?
Be it tiny pond or Pacific symphony, lake of any size, stream,
or trickle
    In its might rivers, lazy slow hypnotic movement
    of precious substance
        each exploration upon land a tad longer

until that fateful day when the dirt,
plants, rocks,
    become shelter, comfortable,
    inhabitable
        but the cellular memory of water
        forever alive

Sheer delight to drink good clean clear water of our
composition
    water hydrates, cleanses, enlivens, provides food,
    bodily functions
        elemental to life on this beautiful blue ball
        called Earth
            earthlings all with fundamental differences
                yet all are drawn to water for
                various reasons
                    the glimmer within water
                    is the light

Are we not all swimming in the liquid crystal light resident
in everything,
    divine stuff of which we are made, move, and have
    our being?
        Igniting a deep sense of unity as if floating in a
            luminosity of sheer delight as when one
            enters a beautiful
                body of water emanating an
                atmosphere of new
                    sweetness, a loving sense
                    of belonging

To the whole of all Creation is this liquid crystal
    divinely created substance
        in which we all may rejoice!

GIFTS OF LOVE AND LIFE

Are you not aware, sense intuit within a feeling,
a withdrawing opening into a new space
where inspiring healthy growth, a freshness is now forming?
Can you not sense the shifting sands of the old, tired
> overused, not working ways imploding
> upon themselves?
> Creating a fungal ground of being vigorous, fresh
> ordained organization
> learning at a new level, hearing the silence's soft
> whispers of truth?

The cacophony of too much so-called information
slowly fading
no longer intriguing, interesting or authentic new
breezes moving
scented by lovely fragrances of kindness and caring,
loving oneself
others caressing your skin, hair roots and all ones very
cellular structure
> A new song is beginning to be heard in the ethers
> touching the receptive soul
> the healing balm of responsibility for one and all
> mending old wounds
> A way of being is birthed among long desired
> awakening peaceable humans

Each receives, perceives in their own way and timely
personal process
like a magnificent garden awakening in springtime,
one plant at a time sprouting, budding, blooming each plant
in its own time
The true feminine aspects once again infused with
beauty, strength

and balanced compassionate power
once dynamic male of thousands of years withering,
shriveling, diminishing
from egoic driven domination to an awakened sense
of true masculinity

Thus, disappearing dioceses, organizations, separations,
divisions,
policies of conflict, barriers to countries and unjust
governments
morphing into a living, breathing organism of unified
oneness
a cooperative partnership a mentality for all living things—
humans, animals,
    earth, sky, waters, plants, ethers, minerals,
    encompassing all the planetary kingdoms
    at last, coming again into harmony, balance, thriving,
    healthy results
    as was the originality of it all once more

A living organism of one people, one living beautiful Mother
Earth from whom everything
in its original form comes forth from Her buxom and
bowels, each living organism
is benefitted by her, everything we eat, drink, wear, use,
drive, reside in are created
from her bounty in raw form a preciousness prevails, gifts
for the good of all
A vivid vision of no divisions, only vibrant, beautiful,
bountiful units of love and light
    All participating in joyous, harmonious productivity
    creating workable lives for all
    at last, not organizational separations but one
    cohesive organism each held
    by the living radiating vibration of pure love, the fabric
    of peaceful life

THE SEED OF HOPE

How precious the moment, how glorious the morning,
how vital is life.
Can you not see the thrust of supreme energy
being exhibited
in valleys, hills, various countries and wee gardens?
What song is being sung in the spheres?
What magic is manifesting in hidden corners
or on random streets all over the world?

Even war-torn lands being desecrated still, a blade
of verdant green
full of hope and promise arises, exhibiting itself to
place a seed
of hope into weary hearts; if untrammeled, the promise
of beauty will burst forth to touch the soul with magic of
knowing there are other forces at work.

Perhaps a whispered prayer erupting from deep within
a wounded one
floats into the ethers to the ear of one who is faithfully
a listener.
Hope like a small seed erupting dawns in the discouraged
heart, a frail faith
forming for a better season, a cessation of war, hatred,
humanities cruelty
to each other fading into a soon yesterday where sanity arises,
a new day to rebuild the hurting hearts from material
devastation

A prayer for all the world, "May the darkest minds be disturbed by a
sliver of light entering, exposing the muck and mire of
egos gone mad
and begin a seeding of transformation like desecrated earth
slowly healing itself to allow life to again be a testimony
    to forces unseen, yet ever present,
    powerful and healing."

The Infinite recreating a living promise of the eternality of all
creation in ever changing, expanding expressions.
Each blade of grass speaks peaceable praise to the majesty
and mystery of the living presence of life Itself, known by many
names and symbols, yet all encapsulated in the
    One Original Seed.

chapter 5

Soulful Sea

SOULFUL SEA

That wonderful pressure on my face, head, bridge top
of nose area, an imprint
Of the Presence, a reminder that each has a third eye
to be opened,
Seeing in a new way, perceiving all that is about us both
physical and non-physical
With new sight, deepening dimension much greater breath ...

The sounds of the morning here at the beach
Are eternal sounds going back beyond time's reach
The song of the surf has a meditative chant
The rolling on shore whispers what can be, not can't

How many ages has this secret been told
Into the hearts of those who walked of olde
And still the same siren sings a song
Of what is right, not what is wrong

Refresh yourself in the morning glisten
For here lies wisdom for those who listen
Is the chant, "You can, you can!"
Repeated, repeated, again and again

For all of life's fortune begins with a peek
One glimpse of what might be
Hear the song the sea sings to me
"You can, you can do good things!"
Strengthened by spirit, inspiration springs

The song of the sea sings not just for me
But for all who will hear the message so dear
Listen not to the hits of the day
For surely in them will come delay
Delay of your dreams, your hopes so high
Listen to the sea and reach for the sky!

What is wanted to be done this day
That is different than the usual way
What new thought can I hold in my heart
What a wonderful dream with one step, a start
The help needed is ever here
Imparting sight so clear
A dream of what one wants to see
Then for sure, answers come to thee

WAVES

What do the waves bring to me?
And what do the waves take away?

Waves this spring morning are so gently lapping upon
the shore
Bringing profound pleasure for years, and years
of joyous anticipation approaching the sea

> Will the waves be high, rough, crashing or rolling?
> Is this a day in which one can swim freely
> and joyously?
> Or a day to be alert and aware while in the realm
> of water?

Oh, the waves, no two are alike, ceaselessly roll upon the
shore delighting my heart
The waves carry away cares of the day, uptight, stress,
confusion, or anger

> Washing over feet, it is as if nerve endings relax
> and let go
> allowing this gift of nature to bathe in loving
> envelopment,
> carrying one to and fro upon its bosom

Yet, the waves have also threatened and frightened my very existence on this planet,
and the gift was the knowingness of complete powerlessness in the embrace of such a force

> It was a shattering and yet an expanding moment
> a few years ago
> When not sure I would ever reach shore alive
> Fear and gratitude danced together within
> exhausted emotions
> Then deep sleep washes over just like the waves.

Deep, deep into an ocean of unconsciousness repose
to healing freedom, profound relief, the sea and the soul
softly sigh

SEASHELLS AND SHESHELLS

Artist date, seashell plucking along the shore
Oh, look, here is one and one more!
Gifts from the sea delivered to me on sandy carpet floor
Each so different in shape and size
Each has coloring to trick the eyes
Each was a home for creature now gone
Each is a sonnet of eternity long

The child in me does love to gather
Pluck and hunt are something I'd rather
Some ancient time I must have been
A gatherer, picker for tribe and kin
I can barely take a walk and not some treasure find
A flower, a plant, a rock, a twig, or some lovely twine
Drag it home to garden, vase or shelf placing a daily find

Somedays, the treasures are not objects found
But thoughts deep, profound arising within
For one idea from the bosom of the Presence
Could make all Earth's riches agree
"You are only one idea away from the riches of the Universe"
A favorite quote from a book, eyes often rehearse

Reminding myself that it is up to me
All of life is essentially free
The air, the sun, the sea, and shore

It is only ego that must have more
A simpler life one could surely live
But what would one have to give?
Old ideas of how it should be in our image

Letting go, just agree that what is wanted is just to BE
Not doing, running, questing "after things" has been our fall
Letting go, living in peace for this could be a life release
Thoughtful ponderings, not do in a rush
Something to meditate, now in a hush

BLESSING TO BLESSING

Blessing to blessing is the true way of life
For all has been already given to you
The Earth is your mother, produces great food
The waters pure and fresh; oceans, too

All has been given for you to enjoy
The beauty to delight your heart
Music of birds and breeze, rivers song
The air ever purifying a splendid start

A wonderful beginning place to praise
For all that has been gifted for life's delight
Guides, angels, teachers and spirit holy
So each can receive inner sight

Spiritually, we are here to care for all of life
The Earth is ever giving of her abundance
The air and the beauty, song and season
All for the rich enjoyment in the dance

So dance a exuberant dance today
Go as a joyous, loving impartation to all you see
this infinite function is elegant,
be a blessing and blessed you'll be

THE GIFTS OF MEMORIES

I remember the beauty of sunsets
so many in a very different setting,
the colors so vivid, the shades so soft
that all rainbows are one rainbow begetting

I remember the beauty of my first-born child
No other was as magnificent as he,
the beauty of my first daughter,
then my second girl, each exquisite to see

I can recall the surging beauty of my first kiss
Was it with you?
All first kisses in a lifetime of kissing
are excitingly beautiful

I remember Paris at day's end,
the lights first beginning to shine
The sunrise of the earth
from Bali's volcano tops, all mine

Beauty of the roses gracing my garden
each more perfect than the one before,
flowers, music, dancers and acrobats
Beauty is everywhere, truly a mystic lore

BEACH REFLECTIONS

The shoreline kisses my feet
    Ocean's body caresses and enfolds
Carrying me on her ever-moving currents —
        Up, down, in, out, undulating rhythm
        Allowing timelessness to
        Tantalizing a deep awareness

THE SEASHELL

Finding this day, an unexpected, beautiful seashell by the road
sensing it was a gift,
feeling it was from source energy, thus valuable

My hand reached down and plucked it up
excited as a child
marveling at its beauty
the many hues of purple, violet, white
also green, plus the creaminess of its smooth center

Reflecting that it was only a half, and that somewhere
out there in the Universe was the other half
perfect fit in solemn recognition
Of the heart longing for that missing other part

An unexpected joy in the receiving of this half shell
that in itself is whole noticing its soft indentation,
making it a receptacle
a receiving vessel to hold
sweet fluid and blessings

Pondering that it is like a heart
open and receptive to that inflow
for the joy, love, peace, exhilarating
expression of the Unseen One

May hearts be open to the good
ready to release all that no longer serves
replaced with that mystical union
the seashell becoming
the sea in me

ANCIENT CHANT — OM NAMA SHIVAYA

The Ancients still chant their vibrational prayer statements
to the Universe
The Aborigines skillfully sing their song lines to the earth
and sky
having done so for perhaps thousands of years
The Tibetan Buddhist of various sects' melodious guttural
voices calling forth
compassion for all sentient beings

Hindu's use their chimes and evoke petitions and prayers for
all the world
Native American tribal people sing, dance and call to the
Four Directions for guidance
Meditators go into the silence and awaiting the whispering
wisdom of mystical voices, past and present.

Those connected to the Ancient Ancestral
Grandmothers cast the
Net of Light for all living things and all the kingdoms
of the Earth
Priests intone the Mass and ceremonies honoring
the Risen Christ
in various multiple languages around the globe

Other believers on their knees petitioning, begging for their
loved ones
and help for survival, food or safety
Jewish traditions recite age old psalm prayers calling upon
a distant
God of the Torah

Metaphysicians affirm prayer treatments for others
and themselves
knowing the Oneness of all with the Infinite Creator

Farmers, gardeners, nature lovers connect with Mother
Earth in
grateful recognition of everything she provides for us all

Do the birds not sing their praise early in the morning?
A lovely concerto divine
Does the Sun not silently rise proudly proclaiming new days
blessings the Life Giver fresh every new morning

Do great whales, dolphins, small fish and large, salt or
fresh waters
not breach to catch the sunshine upon their aquatic bodies?
Surely a celebration of sheer joy to be alive another day
may we not do the same?
Do creatives not quietly access words, music, strokes
of inspiration
from another realm with pencil, pen, brush, or carving tool?

Seeing the evidence of the 'Other' flowing into form
on page, canvas, sculpt or stage?
The inventor witnessing perhaps innovation
to benefit others thus needed for the planet

Does not each soul in some way welcome the newborn hope
of this day
within their heart-mind, at least for an instant?
An acknowledged, something perhaps, as yet
not recognized
but slowly unfolding within them
Sensing an existence of an Unseen Presence, unknown but
inhaling, exhaling breath by breath, gently being revealed

Greeting the day with personal reverence intuiting the very
miracle of being alive,
the gift of one day at a time is surely a true blessing; may we
all see it as so!

A THOUSAND ANGEL FACES

Angels whisper very low
only the quiet can hear.
Angels hover around us all
with loving intent and faces dear.

If we are quiet, so very, very still
encouraging, warming wise words,
we may hear the inspiration that fills.

We are one, we are one,
searching are many; all are connected
such a lovely tranquil gift

THE SEA AND SURFERS

The sea, in her beauty
    and startling diversity
today arose once more
    to support surfers' passions
longing for her sensuous rides
    she has been flat,
        uneventful
        hoarding her ration

But today, the supple
    serpentine movement
of water folding over itself
    creating each exciting swell
the surfing hardy souls
    there rejoicing
        once again
        all is well!

INFINITE PATHS OF LUMINOSITY

Infinite paths of light upon the sea
    call the imaginations towards the horizon
What pathway is calling, pulling the soul towards
    What? Who? Where?
The hypnotic beauty of the trillions of sparkling
gems dancing
    upon the surface of aqua blue ocean
Entices the unsolved riddles within the human psyche

TIDES

The tide energy is lower, but low tides reveal lovely little
tide pools
     of hidden life and a child's delight
Part of the scenario of the mother's waltz through the
seasonal cycles,
     The hide and seek of the Moon pulling, pushing
     planetary currents

An age-old dance, sensitives are affected by these
cosmic changes
     embracing the slow time as well as the rapid
     pace of others
Glide into the day being in harmony with necessary changes
     sunlight caught in glistening jewels upon
     the shallow pools

Energizing small microorganisms and newly spawned baby fish,
     All living things are surf riders on the waves of
     energetic impulses
Within the earth and celestial movements, sway,
sing melodiously
     Dance, sweet souls, with the music of this gift of day

Within higher forces and all that is, nothing is wrong
     There is a Universal Intelligence having set forth
     into motion
The perfect mechanism to balance all life, if undisturbed
     May humanity awaken to the wisdom of age old cycles

Learning again to work harmoniously without needless
destruction
    motivated by selfishness and greed-driven agendas
Simpler, less aggressive actions bring forth lasting results
in both
    the individual life and great expanse of various
    life forms

May all be the contributors to the natural ways
    bring once more, a healthy and harmonious eco system
and an enlightened, thus gratifying soul path for all
    by lovingly tending Earth's bodies of water

UNSEEN PRESENCE

Have you ever felt a kiss upon your cheek
    when no one physical was there?

Have you experienced a tender embrace
    where no visible arms are present?

A moment of whispered endearment
    from somewhere beyond the rational?

Cherish these dear moments
    of being deeply cared for

Just because,
    you are.

MY ALTAR

How many waves have washed upon the shore?
How many sunsets have turned sea and sand golden?
How many footprints were imprinted then washed away?
How many shells have tumbled ashore into the sun?

A gift from the shore, a peek at the eternality of life
How long have sea creatures lived, died, and washed ashore?
At the sea, I see the hand of the divine artist
The creative enormity of the One and so much more

One small shell reveals an intricate design
The Creator bringing forth exquisite expressions
A sea-washed shell, still with sand
Speaks to me of an all-loving hand

SONG OF THE SOUL

In the Universe there is one song that sounds always.
It is the Song of the Source singing into the souls
of humankind;
each soul is a part of the Great Soul and It's song.
Only those who listen will within themselves this music find.

The Song of Compassionate embraces the melody
that sings within each soul who will ever live,
but the song ignored causes aberrant beings
who hear not the compassion for all to give.

It is in the listening deeply that the song is heard.
The sweet music of the soul brings to light
beauty, empathy, joyous love, peace
embracing that One with wisdom from hurtful fall.

Compassion is the salve that heals the wounds
of hurting humanity.
Compassion is the sound that shields humankind
from further humility.

Compassion is an expression of soul,
has nothing to do with religion in part.
The more religious, often less compassion.
Dogma gets stuck in the head missing the heart.

The Song of the Soul brings forth it's gift —
compassion for self and for each other.
Compassion in thinking and being
resulting in harmony for all our sisters and brothers.

A NEW WORLD, BREATH BY BREATH

The ego and the pain body do this terrible dance
Self-righteous indignation, a deathly prance
Until awareness interrupts this tragic trance.

Take a deep breath and then breathe again
For in the breath, access some stillness and space
Awakened to a timeless dimension and an easier pace.

Slowly, breath by breath, awareness by awareness
The reluctant pain body and ego never fully gone, but retreat
Inner space increases, present formlessness and presence meet

BEACH MEDITATION

Face lifted to the sun
    soft belly,
        beautiful naturalness
    in human form

The inner connectedness
    of all life
        sun, sky, air, sea, green growing things
    starfish, shellfish
        various aquatic life
    of earth, moon, stars
        equally as vibrant to drinking in
            the moonlight, stardust
        or sunshine filling my soul with joy
           gratitude
              renewal

SATURDAY

A lovely gray, tidepool morning, clear mini ponds of visible
sea life.
Tide pool mornings are "child still alive in me" mornings,
"Aha dawnings!"

How ancient is the sand shifting upon the shore?
How old are the waters that come gifting allure?
How primordial are the rocks sheltering creatures tiny?
How long covering hidden scurrying things spiney?

How many suns have kissed this strand?
How many moons have shown upon wet sand?
How many ages have come and gone?
How many poets have sung such a song?

The eternal quality of Sun and Moon
The extraordinary constant of night and noon
Countless days have come and gone
Each a potential gift from dark to dawn

What words can express the fervent sigh
Universe that does not die!
Thankful
Truthful
Nature's natural world does not lie!

MAY WE KNOW OURSELVES AS ADORED

Ahh, the bliss
    to know this
Sweet gentle delight
    to be one's own light
Oh, the deep soul satisfaction
    to love as one is loved with passion

One knows by the results
    good things flow, not stuck ruts
Embraced by the joy surrounding me
    and everywhere, that special glow to see
Knowing hand on my hand
    No longer alone, together we stand

May we know ourselves adored
    no longer, these prior hours ignored
Being loved, and oh, cherished
    May this be true, before we perish

THE SHORELINE

The shoreline kisses my feet
Ocean waters caress and enfolds
Carrying me on her ever-moving currents
Up, down, in, out, undulating rhythm
    Allowing
        Timelessness to tantalize my deep awareness

COME AWAY, MY BELOVED, COME

Come away, my beloved and abide with me.
Come away, sweet child, to find refreshment
Come gently down this secret path
That leads faithfully to enduring enrichment.

Come, dear heart, into the silent realm of peacefulness
Quiet that nullifies the stress
Immortal silence stretching
The soul to greater expansiveness.

Come away, weary one, the world will run
Without your ability
There is compensation still unrealized for you
Creativity, moral stability
The touch that makes one inwardly anew.

Come away, my beloved, come away
A sojourn of the soul
Whispers producing expanding brain energy
Things heretofore untold.

Come,
    Come away,
        To the fifth dimension,
           Beloved one,
               Come.

chapter 6

Mysteries

HOW GREAT A MYSTERY

How great a mystery surrounds us —
unseen worlds within unseen worlds.
What eyes must open to see the unseen?
What state of mind allows infinity within?

How many angelics hover nearby?
How many enlightened ones speake?
Oh, ears open to mighty words,
oh, inner spirit open to heavenly sight.

Do I sense you in the morn?
Do I feel you in the dark of night?
In quiet moments, is it your music just beyond my ear?
In simple task, your peace like a breeze, brushes my face.
Is it your power I feel when I need the extra push?
Is it your love when writing or calling to soul laid upon
my heart?
How close is the veil that separates this world from yours?
Will you open a small rip that I may commune
and fellowship?

A student at master's knee,
Opening mind and heart
to learn the truth of all life,
the vast universe and boundless you.

REFLECTIONS –
THE TRUE ESSENCE OF THINGS

Have you not seen the amazingly blue skies after the rain
      reflected into a mud puddle capturing clouds and sky
Somehow the clouds are more mystical as one gazes
upon an image
      than looking up at the same clouds lost in the
      sky's vastness

Ancient structures are awe inspiring and intricately designed
      reflections seem surrealistic and magically alive
Whispering secrets hidden in the cold carved stone,
coming alive
      in the mirrored magnificence revealing missed details

Reflections capture the original into artistic form
      carrying the impressionistic template to the mirror
Capturing body of water, sky, and our own consciousness
      Images, the true intended original divine Creation

It happens often in sacred ceremony calling upon the
Divine Presence
      that the original true self is revealed to the recipient soul
Awakening within their own being who they truly are,
a becoming,
      shedding the persona developed from culture and
      life endeavors

A soft unseen whispering of higher trust radiates through
the body
      to the listening heart, answers heretofore unknown
      are revealed
The holy essence of the person, true divine creation is
brought forth
      into focus of one's soul-purpose on this life's
      inspired pathway

You are that which has ordained you to be now and forever
      you are loved, held, helped, surrounded by
      unseen witnesses
Ancient ancestors, ascended masters, angelics, and
elementals
      all here to assist our walk upon this earth needing care

May we see the holiness reflected in every form, each
living thing
      back of every countenance, moving in every experience
The deepening refraction passes through confusion
of Human actions,
      nothing is nearer to us than the essence of our own
      true being

MYSTERIES AND SURPRISES

This day like any other yet filled with mysteries
and surprises.
She goes forth aware of the unseen miracles asking
little attention
yet are right in the scheme of movement of life
on this planet.
Circulation of air currents, without which none would live.
Air streaming off the ocean bringing ions necessary
for survival and enjoyment.

Water running in lakes, streams, underground currents,
ponds and wells.
Mighty rivers, springs, rain, snow and ice all furnishing
the Planet
with the needed moisture to grow crops that sustain life.
Abundance of plums on tree outside the window all from
the generosity
of water, air, soil, sunlight each given from the heart
of generosity.

Light is our joy; moon is a glow for dreaming.
Earth itself—soil, dirt growing every kind of green,
nourishing plant
for sustaining aliveness of humans, animals, birds and all.
The entire food chain comes from the earth.
It truly is our mother; food and water are mother's milk
to humankind.

Be it simple rice, beans or gourmet morsels; all come from
the same fungal
source, the dirt beneath to be blessed, praised
and protected.
Mysteries, surprises appear each day in the wonder
of nature unfolding all about.
All these bounties are freely given from the source of all life.
Miracles that barely call for acknowledgement

This day great gratitude pours forth from a thankful heart.
A freedom of seeing all that has been generously given
            declaring thankfully, "I am a good receiver."

STEPS ON LIFE PATH

Steps to solutions
Steps to understand life path
Steps are the building blocks of a life
    One step, one breath, one day
    creates footsteps in the sand of
    one's soul walk while upon the earth

No escalators, trains, planes, or any vehicle
except the human foot, from first step to last,
there is only one mental engineer
    that runs the movement
    of each thought, and actions
    create the footprint; there is no other

Each is the chooser and the chosen
No matter the intellect, extraordinary or diminished
choice still initiates the mental chooser
    Consciously, deliberately, or
    unconsciously, careless, or uncaring
    All still make their own imprint upon the path
    which becomes the road

Yet, pathways can be changed or corrected
New territories explored resulting in a higher road taken
All lives have opportunities to choose and rechoose
    Often as simple as a definite "yes" or "no"
    both words are a complete sentence
    steering the compass of an individualized life

A lull, a quiet
All are eventually presented with a fork in the road
The decision marks the destination which creates destiny
 Step by step repeatedly, becomes the road
 There is no other way but a foot stretching forth in
 desired direction
 One breath, one intention, one willing, inquiring,
 faithful step at a time
 Seemingly the mystical becomes each soul's life path

MY GOD IS THERE

It is a comfortable thing to feel confident on my knees
    in the church of my youth
It is a delightful thing to feel welcome in temple, cathedral
    or Glastonbury's altar

It is a marvelous thing to light a candle white
    tapered and long
To think of my community and family
    both here and now gone

It is a splendid thing to know
    with great peace we are one
We are one, and in me,
    holy beloveds, release

No barriers, no taboos or who is
    right or wrong
For on this planet, as God's child,
    I belong!

Burn my white candle
    purchased with love and good thought
Your flame, oh my candle, is my prayer
    that through light spirit is sought

Bless each dear one with seed that will grow
in the silence of holiness, one day will show
Being at home in temple or shrine,
grotto or cave; in all, light doth shine

Many expressions of one reverent prayer
that love be the portion, free of despair
All hearts in the silence whispered the same prayer
that we will be protected and loved with care

So, we must love each one that we meet
the Divine is in everyone on every street
No matter the numerous travel I share
My God is there, my God is there!

THE ANGEL AT THE DOOR

There is a door within us all
Not seen but hidden, not too tall
This door has an angel waiting there
To guide your passage when you dare

"Behold," I stand at the door and knock
This spoken by the Eternal Rock
The one on whom all can rely
The one speaking truth, never a lie

When you approach with ready heart
That is the moment the door will part
An angel helps you through the door
Then Spirit in love shows you more

Here is one greater than all, here is your reason
no need to stall for within your very being
Is the door with angels singing your answers, your path,
your very life finding your true self that knows no strife

Open the door each and every day
That is the moment your heart does pray
Here is the light to shine within
Allowing the means to live beyond whim

Each has a chamber deep inside
Each has a destiny busyness will hide
Thus, only time in quiet prayer
Opens the door to riches there

Your angel beckons, "Come today"
Your new life is only a prayer away
Angels rejoice in heavenly song
When one heart bows, resisting so long

REFLECTIONS

Reflections, refractive, refractions
What I see, do I truly see?
What I perceive, is it real?

Reflections in the mirror
are all backwards to what is.
Is that I see the real deal?

Reflections of my mind
Did I recall the way it was or is,
or do my own perceptions steal?

The looking glass upon my desk
reflects the trees and hills outside
Is it as all appears as real?

Is it only an illusion in the glass
captured by paint and light
...refractions of what I think I see?

How much of my life is real or illusion?
How much of my thinking is my own?
How many beliefs are refractions of others?

Papers, movies, television and talk radio
all paint a picture upon the screen of the mind.
What is false, perhaps the real smothers.

An illusion, all illustrations of my own making
I truly am the creator in my world
blaming no others, certainly not mothers.

What we have created we can re-create.
We can paint over any canvas in our mind
until our desired reality appears, not another.

Then, truly we are the co-creative divinity in our world.
The reflections are of our own making.
Using deeper knowing, allows mystery to be uncovered.

COURAGE TO PREVAIL

Courage comes in tiny drops of preparation
Gathering your facts, putting all in a row
Courage comes by taking tiny steps each day
Until clear in your thinking you know

Courage is not easy for some
It comes with hard won discipline
By doing the tasks one does not like
Necessary effort in order to win

So do your tasks and be at peace
Be clear in your own mind
When the moment of confrontation arises
A blessing there you may find.

DEDICATED LIFE, SACRED TIME

Honoring the dedication to one's sacred time, sitting
in the fresh air of a
    new day by the front door most mornings
A dedicated practice of writing thoughts, concerns, prayers
and listening
    consistency creates a life of ingrained habits,
    practices, results
A daily walk, casting Net of Light prayerfully for all living
things, all the
    kingdoms of air, earth, fire, waters, animals, plants,
    humans, angels,
        ancestors, divas, elementals, minerals upon and
        beneath earth
            home, garden, friends, family, business
            all touched

A dedicated life gives structure, sanity and inner sense
of participating
    in the good for all, known and unknown,
    countries, cosmos
Achievements come from a solid routine of taking steps
in the direction of
    our dreams, intentions, and highest aspirations
    for the planet
Life presents many pathways, forks in the road, right or left,
hills or even
    terrains, mountains to climb, valleys to transverse,
    all lives have low
        lands of exploration, also the meadows
        of green grass,
            wildflowers arrayed so rare, lovely designed
            handmade carpet

All are a part of the mystery journey and if embraced
enriching the tapestry woven
    by each day, perhaps mundane routine, or times of
    high creativity
Success, love, and laughter all experiences give
a special texture
    to the display we call life
Each unique by the chosen avenues of activities, silent
times, companions,
    work we chose and often the locale in which we live;
    humans are
        somehow shaped by the space they occupy, yet
        also have the
            ability of mobility to change and redirect
            one's direction

Many various steps which become life decisions, or not, create
    new pathways or patterns by entering into a different
    human experience
Hopefully enriching and in unison with the universal
soul expansion
    which is ever evolving, reflecting the cosmos progression
Then perhaps decline thru regression of human actions
    as history has shown again and again
        Each and every human life is a mini
        cosmological entity
            breath by breath, step by step, each day
                as sure as the Sun faithfully rises with
                the blessings of
                    the Divine Creator fresh and new
                    every morning

THE UNSEEN LIFE

Life, while plain is peaceful
uneventful, yet rich in kindness
helpful hands and conversations
smiles, kind words
    feeling loved,
        enriching

Small garden gifting daily
herbs, greens, vivid tomatoes red
flowers, perfume, beauty alive and new
birds freely singing in sync with wind chimes
    enjoying

Friends reach out on phone or email
Facebook greetings, emails
not noteworthy but endearing
invitations, groups, communities, relationships
    connecting

Aloneness is a state of mind
unseen companions present all our lives
not heard, visible, but sweetly felt
    friends physical and those unseen

PEACE IN THE HOOD

if we want peace on the planet
let us begin in our neighborhood
neighbor furious with neighbor
harboring injuries perceived as rude

one against the other
my rights, no mine
on and on go the stories
until no light will shine

hatred and anger are heavy foes
they dampen the most beautiful day
anger and prejudice are foul partners
retelling and telling what this one did say

where is peace on earth
and good will to humankind?
If I cannot find it in my hood
it is nowhere else for me to find

it begins here, right here within me
I must put away the days of old
and try to find forgiveness and release
no matter what story is told

peace on the Earth, goodwill to all
that is the song we often sing
but unless we bring it into our experience
it is a cold, empty, meaningless thing

may I begin right where I am
anger and hatred now replace
may good will and kind thoughts
to bring peace upon this place

EPOCHS OF TIME

The epochs of time like waves, washing over humanity
Waves of plenty, waves of waste
Rolling waters of war, then sweet tides of peace
Is it the energetic thought patterns of humankind
that influence
    the variance of human history?
    What else can it be?

In the Torah of olde when a righteous ruler reigned,
peace prevailed,
Crops flourished and the people enjoyed the gift of
a pleasant life
Worshipping the omnipotent omnipresent Creator by
multiple names
When an unbalanced ego driven king or ruler had control
of the reins
    of a country, war ensued, famine often came
    upon the land
    The men were engaged defending leaving
    families alone

Misery multiplied until at last the unjust authority
was displaced
How often the clever-tongued candidate with enticing
promises and
pompous posturing of strength, not caring for citizens
or country

Deceiving by lies, yet then rewarded with the keys
to the kingdom
Self-servicing hidden agendas eventually come forth after
gathering those
of the same ilk around this figurehead
Soon where peace and harmony once upon the land,
divisiveness,
      rancor and hardships become the way causing
      the Earth
      and the populace to suffer unnecessary sorrows

Are we blinded by our own selfish desires?
Seeing an opportunity to prosper even at the expense
of the deprivation of those less fortunate? It would seem so
      The people become downtrodden, the environment
      and earth are
      uncared for and very often drastically harmed

People curse their god who had graciously bestowed upon
all people
the responsibility and gift of volition, free choice without
intervention
Thus, humanity creates human woes through the lack
of loving unity,
cooperatively working together for the good of all, not just
those who
      belong, preaching exclusion rather than inclusion

Even the Great Divine becomes an accoutrement to be
paraded as influence,
rather than a heartfelt unifying spiritual element
not desiring the good of all, just those like us. There is no
other, only we.
No wonder when division is within hearts and minds, the
divisiveness must manifest as the populist
the world is harmed by not lovingly fairly working
for all living beings but it must begin with me

Am I not you and you me, united spiritually in the great
fabric of life?
Separation the evil epoch has long been, must it ever be?
May the vicissitudes of time shift to the mystical original plan
For all living beings endowed with love, joy, peace
abundance, and sweet harmony

BE

Be that which you desire to be
Be the love you desire, for you came from love
Be joyous, for you are a good idea in God's mind
Conceived in joy and love
Be filled with the spirit of peace inside you'll find

Be a light one day at a time
Knowing your divine journey is many days
Bring light and see darkness flee
For the light within can penetrate any haze

Be prosperous for you were born rich
Children of the king of kings are you
The Father has given you the kingdom
Only you can stifle the flow of what is due

The kingdom is within you
So adorn it richly as you dare
Beauty and opalescence are for you
Your treasure within is your lair

If you believe it you shall have it
owning it as it is so, it shall be
Life is what you declare it is
Act like the Beloved and see!

SACRED CYCLICAL DANCE

Sacred Sunday morning
Sunshine and bird songs
Moist earth from welcome rain
Life is good in this moment

The wonder of green leaf stalks
Penetrating inside earth into light
Bulbs hibernating harvesting energy
Bursting into sight
Fragrant flowers to follow

This is the wonderous life cycle
Deep sleep, re-birth into a new day
Cycles dancing within soul circles
Calling those onto itself
No accident, recognition of each
Circles within circles know their own

Mystics speak of these wonderous whirls
How quickly we seem to forget
Yet recognition almost instantly
Attraction like an old friend new

Each year, bulbs sprout and grow
Yet never the same in time
Usually, spring, this year fall
They hear music calling them forth

A life can change in a day
A season, year or decade
Like some magnetic force attracting
People, events, occurrences,
Familiar and yet new faces

Who orchestrates these things?
Who says who is to come and then go?
What symphony plays to which we dance?
A new day, what will now unfold?
Sacred cyclical dance

WHY IS THERE FEAR OF DEATH?

What dread hangs heavily upon the heart-mind
    regarding that which is called death?
Is it the unknown, the seeming lack of physical proof
    of a hereafter or heavenly destination?
Or is it the ending of hopes, dreams, desired experiences
    or leaving beloveds, friends, predicable familiarity?

Is it not our own leaving the planet looming large,
    perhaps the witnessing of a dear one's preparations?
Is it we fear the mystery of the solo journey?
    Could it be our own longing for them to stay with us?
An unexpressed guilt of all we could of, would have done
    for them at pivotal times in life?

Maybe a discomfort at core, a self-seeking desiring their
    energetic presence in our lives and not wanting the void?
There are many tangled emotions when separation appears
    Loss is hard for humans to accept or carry emotionally
The heaviness of heart is a crushing load large;
    sadness, perhaps depression visits for a season

We have higher thoughts and say we believe
        yet fear raises its tormented face
Fear of what? Fear of whom? Fearing the unknown?
        Trust leaks away like air from a tired balloon
Faith is revealed as shaky perhaps or not yet a full orb
        Where does inner peace, harmony, acceptance go?

In silent quiet times of surrender into the unseen presence
        that presence, that witness, that guiding force
The quiet, soft and gentle voice that speaks with sincerity
        that has been present all our lives
To the honest questions, the cry of the pure heart,
        a non-grasping inquiry to know one's deeper truth

In facing the vicissitudes of life's challenges
        ask in meditative silence, then hear and know
A settling grace-filled answer bringing acceptance
        that every soul has its own journey
The whys and wherefores are unknown to us
        as humans are not ours to fully understand
Fear not, dear ones, I am with you always

chapter 7

Mystical Moments

SONG OF THE ANCIENTS

Middle of the night meditation:

Behind me, they stand like shadowy, not quite clear figures
A long line of ancestral grandparents
    sending their accumulated wisdom
    strength and sacred thought
    collectively forward to those of us standing in this
    pivotal time

Their wisdom distilled by their toil, tears, loving through
many varying lifetimes,
experiences, ravages, triumphs, these ancient ones and more
    closely related presences sending support and
    encouragement into
    a world desperate for the light gleaned
    through galaxies both near and far

These souls come now to us at this time to champion
The arising Workers of Light with
    song, dance, expanding shifts in the cosmology
    long entranced upon the masculine structures
    created on Earth

The foundations are crumbling as the songs of the sacred
feminine voices arise to see the walls tumble like Jericho
of olde prayer
>   praise power from centuries of yin energies stored,
>   collecting now
>   being mystically channeled through those listening
>   receptacles
>   of re-balancing energies

Millions of Soul Lights igniting around the planet shifting
at unseen levels
Strengths that are now appearing in form and positioning
as they chant into a new day
>   "Listen! Listen to the Ancient Ones!"

Many children now entering through women's sacred bowls
are dedicated
karmic-free individual souls coming to assist in helping
to bring forth a new
>   creative society, a world that endeavors to work for all
>   not the greedy few grasping for goods and power,
>   a planet where all are honored, empowered as holy souls

GUARDIANS OF ALL

The old ones say there are spirit guardians for all living things
The Talmud says every blade of grass has a guardian
whispering,
    "Grow, grow, grow…"

Sherpas in the Himalayas speak of the great mountain spirits
Luther Burbank, the respected horticulturist spoke to plants and
    modified their genetic makeup, included creating
    thornless
    cactus and new variety of his famous roses

From the beginning, the verbal legacy of stories and songs
told of trees
that spoke and plants that miraculously appeared
    In Glastonbury, England, the ancient thorn bush
    blooms twice a year,
        around Christmas and Easter to memorialize the
        risen Christ

Great ones have meditated under the Bodi Tree and found
enlightenment
beneath that sacred old growth yet alive sheltering presence
    whispering truths that have shaped a people

The Great Teacher Jesus communed in the garden
of Gethsemane for
courage to carry forward, to face the awaiting cruel passion
of crucifixion
>   Sacred plants, frankincense and myrrh were his first
>   gifts from wise men

The Christian scriptures as well as others speak
of angelic presences
appearing as guardian angels for each newborn
and also foretelling
>   of a child to come to presumed barren women

In olde Erin, many have seen the little people hiding among
the blossoms
and leaves in the woodlands, thickets, and cottage gardens
>   In other parts of the Isle gnomes are a mischievous
>   part of common thinking
>   Fairies have been spotted all over the world for untold
>   passage of time

Divas, elementals are known to inhabit stands of great
redwoods
primordial forests, many passionate gardeners sense and feel
>   unseen presences, such as those nurturing
>   both the twining roses and olde precious lemon tree

CONDUIT

It comes not from me
I am only the conduit
The flow from Source
to those who come near
It is not me, but Thee
that speaks a word
that encourages or lifts
those near to me so dear

It is not my wisdom
or even my love
I am only a conduit
willing to be a vehicle small.

To all that should come my way
by unseen appointment
It is my purpose to source
higher love to those who call

This depletes nothing in me
for it comes not from me
but mystically thee,
for the fullness is always
the One
         I cannot see

PROFOUND UNION

In the hours of darkness
    when my soul doth travel
Calling to those with whom
    one longs to mingle
Do they not then appear in
    my life?
Arriving like a spring flower
    a beauty single?

For each flower is unique
    yet similar
So is each soul journey in
    search of answers
Calling through mystical
    shining spheres
Waiting silently for an
    appearance now due

Are not all oceans
    one ocean?
Do not all rivers run
    to the sea?
Do not all tears come from
    the same soul sorrow?
Is infinity not searching in
    the depth for me?

Are we not bone of
    the same bone?
Flesh of all flesh
    in differing hues?
Are You not everywhere,
    and nowhere?
Traveling the Heavens, calling
    profoundly united at last

CREATION STORY - COSMIC WEB

Father God was most busy creating earths, planets, stars, moons,
    galaxies, and oh so much more
Mother God was engaged in crocheting an intricate lace
web spread
    throughout the entire cosmology holding all
Together they laughed and planned, visioned, and
schemed plants,
    animals, shapes, sizes, colors, form coverings
    of every kind

She, championing the wonders of Creation in its magnificent
    especially the light piercing into every
    shadowed darkness
The suns, moons, stars, light beings dancing in perfect
rotation
    a brilliant display of coloration, luminosity of sunrises
    and sunsets
He was dazzled by the intricate handiwork cast throughout
the furthest
    reaches of what is called outer space and beyond

Outward, inward, above, below the web of life's weavings
cast into every aspect
    of this newly forming creation executed with great beauty
Energy sent forth emanated from the Jewel of their hearts
    vibrating with loving intentionality, enlivening all
    living things
How jubilantly they marveled at all that had come forth
from the vast
    creativity of mother father god manifesting the
    Oneness of all

The lacework of life, so beautifully made, each pattern
more intricately
        designed then the last
Spanning the entire Universe, a cosmic work, Web of Life,
Net of Light
        handiwork of divine creators holding all
The vast expanse woven in geometric patterning of
unfathomable beauty
        intelligence, the Cosmic Web, Nedra's Net, known
        by the ancients

The largest construct, the first of creation, eternal in
its existence,
        holy, vital, present in all, none excluded every
        form included
Alive, holding planet Earth steady upon its axis, holding
all who call
        upon this Net of Light steady within their own core
Present everywhere throughout the furthest reaches of
all the galaxies
        known and unknown into mystical Infinity.

Footnote: Scientists discovered this fabric/net/web of life in 1980.
Photos can be seen on the Internet as cosmic net.

THE FAR REACH

Our arms cannot reach to the troubled places in the world,
the unjust invasion upon a people not wanting conflict but to
live life, love their families, till the ground, be productive
and enjoy
What does the far away observer do to be supportive and
of value?

Prayers are on the lips of many all over the planet in loving
solidarity
This energetic vibration entering the fabric of all life resounds
subtle unseen yet powerful in truth, binding all together
in Creation

Within each living human there is a soul seed awaiting
awakening,
nurturing, attention from which a ground of being
is established
holding that even the most aggressive warlike humans
still have an
unacknowledged part of their being that longs to awaken

The one spirit incarnate in all, the immortal Presence willing
to expand into
its true magnificence ordained from the Dawn of Creation
affirming this beneficent action emerges, a discovery of the
hidden self

The power back of everything and everyone is ever present,
willing to bestow the cause of all life, all aspirations,
though now seen through a glass darkly a single swipe
allows light
to enter beginning expansion and growth

Is this not the unseen arm that can reach anywhere anytime,
forever available to the call of the heart?
It is said, "Those that live by the sword will die by the
sword," versus
Remembering that the one who loves the most lives the most.

CIRCLE OF LIFE

The circle of life, silently swirling energies of the Universe
Ever moving air with fresh currents like a vortex circulating
in the eternal
spiral circling from smaller movement to a great twirling dance
The energy animating air streams feeding the atmosphere
then like
> bubbling waters in a spa flowing in riotously foam
> and ripples out
>> into the whole awaiting atmosphere.

Is this not like humanities existence upon this lovely
green blue multiple colored planet?
Human DNA circulating from the vortex of male semen into the
> fertile seed chamber of the female's sacred bowl
>> creating new life again and again.

The cross pollination of the human race has seeded and
reseeded the
growing tribes and nomadic wanders from the beginning of time
So that now all peoples everywhere are carrying the same
basic DNA,
one human race, one people with individualized numerical
sequences
> making the amazing arrays of hues, sizes, elegant eyes,
>> myriad shades of differing hair, features, stature
>> yet all one.

Each person created from the One Eternal Source with
varying beliefs,
customs, traditions, foods, dress, songs, dance, languages
An array of the various names of countries and territories,
yet only
     one Earth, with an unlimited variety of fascinating parade
        of the Divine appearing in human form.

Same spectacular scenario in the animal kingdom, plant
world, minerals,
all forms of living things from one Infinite Source
Expanding, morphing, evolving over eons of time, centuries
of circulating
far and wide, creating multiple variety of ever-changing
life forms
     How marvelous all one, yet untold unique miracles
     of life through
         the universal rhythm of spiritual unfoldment
           the very wonder of Life itself

PONDERING HOW IT ALL BEGAN

Lovely, glorious morning, a gift of universal sparkling
beauty of Earth
How did it look that first day of Creation
before birthing of fungi's creepers, mammoth, and minis
upon the planet
barren of green growing vegetation so lushly verdant
from mighty towering tree to the tiny yellow buttercup

It is difficult to imagine the process of evolving eons
What chemical caldron brought forth compounds to
stimulate alchemy?
Some say human life in some form has been transgressing
the earth
for over 180,000 years or more leaving traces
of their existence

Knowing great life roamed ravishing, leaving their
dinosauric remains
embedded upon the tumultuous upheaval of fire
and mayhem
Remains captured for humanity to unearth, dredge from
deep waters
or tar pits, caught in lava and stony hardened mud

Also, to be uncovered, flora, fauna, ferns, sea life and so
much more
　　　Now science is discovering viruses and DNA
　　　unknown before
opening minds to ponder and explore what once was and the
　　　transmigrations of all living forms of life's immense
　　　expressions

Now taken so for granted but still the wonder of miraculous
life, death,
　　　survival and testimonies left behind in the remains
To think it has always been thus or that humanity has not
progressed,
　　　regressed and grappled with survival since the
　　　beginning of what we
call time is naïve

A lovely morning to walk in awe of all the eye can see
　　　silently pondering how many soul journeys to earth
to learn, grow, fail or succeed
　　　and the mind grasping to glimpse upon
the creative genius of life itself

BE STILL

Be still, retire, let go and know the Holy Ones shall run the world
   hold the Earth in prayerful embrace
      keep coming back to source energy
         We will evaluate and communicate what needs
            to be known—what to do, how to do it,
               most importantly how to be

Actions are generated by a higher vibrational energy than
   political, religious, doctrinal, or human agendas
      It will be the unseen forces that move the air, the Sun,
         the Moon, the stars, and shift old,
            trapped thinking

The power that rotates the Earth, changes weather, that is
ever moving,
      creating and re-creating forces greater than the
         human consciousness, yet working through those
            with open, listening hearts

Think of jump time when out of the Dark Ages the
   Age of Enlightenment swept across the ends of
   civilization
         activating new kinds of art, music,
         change everywhere
            the Renaissance was born.

Gifts given in that period are still enlightening,
delighting people
      Great works of art and music, inventions,
           lovely cathedrals
               and stunning architecture

This is spirit working within so that no one in future need
      do without a world that works for all,
           knowing the laws of consciousness,
           what we consistently
               think about shall come about

May our vision and understanding of the fabric of light
      expand within each and all of humanity
           Are not the lay lines on the planet
           always running
               unseen yet stimulating earth's currents
Just as the soul life within can touch, heal, move, and
enlighten those
      who call upon the sacred unity within themselves?

NATURE'S BALLERINA

Where will April go, arriving like a ballerina on pirouetting toes
    casting forth blossoms and blooms of unimaginable
    radiance
A soft concerto of breeze and birds accompanying with
classical clarity,
    music for a dance of spring awakening,
    a mystical moment

Now, so soon, you in almost full expression, leaps, and
riveting movements
    of beauty and grace for these too short passing days
Soon you will bow to a standing ovation heralded by lovers
of nature,
    and me, as you introduce a young vital May to come
    melodiously in

Your talisman of delicate yin energetic impartation remains
in hidden spots
    in the garden and flourishing fields
You, my lovely lady of Mother Nature's bounty, are forever
imprinted into
    the magnificent tapestry of all of earth, season by season

You have swollen hearts and delighted our senses by
putting a new
    awakening love of all the multiplicity evidenced each day
Gifting individually beautiful flowers, small fruitage forming
with leaves so
    generously green to adorn the earth with these
    fragile artworks

Your soft gentle beauty makes you the princess of the seasons,
     a debutante rare, loved by most, now a slight sadness
     to say farewell
Turning our eyes to welcome the yang of May bustling forth
with brisk
     warmer breeze ripening fruit, bringing forth hardier
     flora and fauna.

Farewell, dear beautiful teacher, magical dancer, our spring
ballerina,
     leaving seeds of promise for next year's
     celebratory arrival
Gratitude flows, deep awe inspired by appreciation for
your profound
     performance this season, as you seductively dance away

REJOICING IN THE TORAH

I rejoice in the sacred literature that has lifted humankind
The words that take root and grow within
Inspirational writings that expand one's thoughts
Are the living breath of God causing new life to begin

A thought grasped by a hungry mind
Stretches it to new proportions
Once stretched it can never return
To its former meager intentions

The word of truth is quick and sure
Dividing the bone from the marrow
It is alive, working like yeast in bread
When eaten, alleviating human sorrow

Sorrow from wrong thinking and doing
Sorrow from loss and disappointments here
Sorrow caused by anger and resentment
Sorrows soothed by truth's healing balm, dear

The sacred writings are our treasure
The gifted stories from tribes and clan
Wise holy spirited words
Aiding humankind overcome — we can!

SONG OF THE SPHERES

A refined beautiful simplicity now arises to heal Mother
Earth restoring balance
between both the necessary Yang and Yin, male and female,
all are needing to cooperate with interior parts being
brought by the unseen
  into harmony, the mystical reflected plentitude
  into the workings
  of the entire world, its various peoples,
  balance, symmetry,
  finally, peace for every living thing

This is the Song of the Spheres being sung into our Universe
  to enter hearts and minds by the long line of ancestors
  standing strongly behind us in varying shapes and
  soul expressions vibrating at a new intensity

Shattering the old so that the new ancient Wisdom
may come forth
as the grandmothers of olde hear the crying of the children
have come
  to help, to love, mending the torn fabric of the world
  bringing it back to equality of mutual caring
  and sharing

The way of ancient wisdom in modern adornment regal,
poised, gracious
most powerful, loving, resulting in equilibrium in the
natural world
> a healthy ebb and flow of mutual cooperative support
> Show us the way, light our path, singing your songs
> Chant melodies through us out into every corner of
> the Earth

We are ready to tip the scales of imbalance into a planet
where all
can live in safety, harmony, work to do to care for our
own beloveds
helping others, heals our hearts and minds
> Gratitude flows to all those who have proceeded us
> knowing we are never alone, supported by countless
> Unseen Witnesses

Sing, Ancient Ones! Sing the song of our freedom!

CIRCLES

The moon carves the cosmic circle
The Sun rises and sets in concentric circles
The Earth spins ceaselessly in circles
    We are being twirled

The hands of the clock crawl in circles
The ocean tides flow around and around,
The globe turns in streams of circles
    We wonder why we are confused

 Politicians spin through their speeches
Radios blare their circular disks
Television is nothing but round dots
    Sending reality in spirals

Water runs down the drain in circles
Sometimes left or other right
Depending what part of the planetary arc
    Does gravity also spin in circles?

Circles are the shapes made by the Ancients
Found in round monolithic mounds and rocks
Prehistoric cave markings, pottery has spirals
    Seeming to know no beginning or end

Wedding rings are round
Testifying to forever after
Again, supposedly seamless flow
    Circle symbols everywhere

Orifices, eyes, holes are round
Breasts and babies' mouths
Etc. etc. Use your own images
    Circumferences of your choice

Metaphysicians say we are in soul circles
Revisiting familiar tribe, family, or society
We come, go, circles within circles colliding
    Explains why humanity often is disoriented

SILENT CHIMES

There are times when chimes do not ring
Drums sit in solemn silence
Pianos playing no vibrational notes

Moments when no breeze blows
The stirring of leaves seems still
Even some mornings the birds cease singing

It is well when no words tumble upon the page
Embrace the stillness until another time
Feeling wordless without a spark to write

Even the sea at times appears in repose
Rest your mind and feast upon the sweet silence
Animation of imagination will stir another day

Embracing the now, finding sweet peace

OH, BELOVED I WOULD GIVE THEE

I would awaken a flock of nightingales
to sing love's song for you.
I would herald the gentlest
first ray of the Sun to kiss your face.

I would send the perfume of
a thousand roses to invade
your senses with sweet aroma.
I would wrap you in angels' wings
and carry you to a far-off place.

My dear child, I have created
all these things and more for you,
yet all I desire is daily communication.
I ask you to come commune.

chapter 8

The Light and All
That Is

ONE ILLUMINATING SOURCE

The light you love, loves you, infusing, vitalizing, inspiring
    this Divine Source of life energy being so ample
        graciously given to all Creation

The first audible word spoken out of the seeming void
    into the darkness causing
        dawn to be birthed into the Great Expanse

"Let there be light" resounding throughout the Cosmos
    and there was radiance penetrating, eschewing
        the void of darkness by great rays of light

Life began with miniscule, almost invisible organisms
    awakened beginning the great chain
        of evolutionary building blocks

The voice of the infinite still echoing throughout
    the entire cosmological vastness
        "Let there be light" and so there must be!

May the light in all humanity ever increase
    Chasing the shadows of dark emptiness in hearts,
        Minds, unintentional actions of the
        lower vibrations

May shadows flee forever into the eternal realm
of transformation until what once lurked
in dark consciousness is purified

Becoming transparent like facets
in a priceless jewel reflecting beauty,
harmony and glorious manifestation

The celestial call of reflection to all Creation
"Let your light so shine emanating
from one illuminating source!"

LOSSES AND GAINS – THIS OLDE TREE

When my days are fully expressed
  and sharing of my soul no longer appearing on the page
    this sacred sight of generational memories
      shall lovingly be placed for safe keeping
        into the hands of my children
          a legacy gift for expanding family

There is a special light vibration permeating this tiny dab
  of earth sacred to our hearts and minds again, teaching
    life has beauty and ugly, sweet and tart,
      tears as well as laughter,
        opposites seemingly resident
         in the human pilgrimage

Yet, held correctly with simple grace
  mindfully creating a life
    with beauty and poise
      learning from losses and gains
        embracing acceptance of
         both lemons and roses
         in the tree of life

AURA OF ILLUMINATION

A dull day is fine, a light blazing continuously burns out faster
        The lulls are as important as the brilliant glowing times
Ride the surf break as it comes; it cannot be controlled

The Universe has its own living rhythm, and all are just guests
        Being mellow is good for the body, mind and emotions
Life is like a merry-go-round, up and down, round and round

As the Earth spins on its axis held firmly by the living web of life,
        thus, the planets are so held
Feel the arms of sweet caress holding you in its divine embrace

Gently filling the empty spaces with holy presences
and vibrations
        bask in the unseen love extended to all
Hear the melodious song of kind whispers spoken into
the ethers

More precious than mink or ermine, more lasting than any
brief encounter
        this is the womb of your being into which you arrived
        eons ago
encapsulating you always, you are never without this aura
of illumination

Your aura penetrating, surrounding, seeping into every pore
or empty place
    fill yourself with this light touch from the infinite
    loving presence
available always for you and all living things
Know it, embrace it, own for yourself and all you care for,
meet or touch
    thus, the torch is passed to others on an invisible, yet
    deeply sensed
intuitive opening accepted one by one

A lighted candle lovingly shared in community
    by vibrationally intentional thought, words and
    actions, bring
forth miraculous illumination of the sacred aura
of all Creation

NET OF LIGHT

Vortexes, energy spots, which are something the ancients
    understood, thus built magnificent stone structures
        On many revered sites upon the planet by using the
           crossing currents of the powerful lay lines

These lines are still carrying energy running throughout
the planet
    as the Net of Light fills Creation, an expanded vision
    like running lay lines
        also are in the air currents where heightened
        revelatory thinking,
           creativity comes to all habituated listeners

These ideas are not new, understood by the wise ones since the
    beginning of human existence on this glorious planet
        Meditation is listening, being in the silence, the quiet
           hearing with every cell of one's body

A pure deep knowing beyond the mental strategic mind
    is allowed to come forth not all see visions,
        not all hear voices, not all feel and sense these
        unseen forces inherent in all beings

The quiet contemplation is deep, important work
    This is the means of shifting the power structures
    of human
        thought constructs destroying the planet
           Old things shall pass away, new
           things appear

This is the work of creating new paradigms
    The more praying souls joined together in
    mind connection
        The greater the force for healing, reconciliation,
            freedom, and at long last, peace

It is the way, and it is happening in the collective morphemic
    fields all over the earth, soul by soul
        Each is to do their own interior work and the Holy
            One Presence does the miraculous
            silent shifting

This our ancients practiced knowing
    Shared ideas grow stronger
        Energetic love multiplies within the Net of Light
            holding us all, and our planet steady on its axis.

LOVE IS LIGHT – LIGHT IS LOVE

A day of light and love
    caring and sharing
        blessing and being blessed
            Life is light – even in the darkness light
            is alive
                active and accelerating the
                Infinite Energy
                    through every atom, molecule
                    on this planet and beyond

Enhancing life, light is like electricity always pulsating,
radiating
    throughout the earth into the cosmos
        like air – different densities but always available
            Our human part is to accept, breathe, open
            to the light with
                one whole heart-minds, to connect
                more fully with Divine Source
                    even if one does not open their
                    conscious connection
                        there is receiving,
                        breathing, warming
                        supportive activity

To participate embrace and consciously partake makes living
more alive
    glowing, a daily joy to appreciate the gifts of life,
    nature, the elements
        air-sky, waters of every shape and taste, earth in

all its immense diversity
fire within giving warmth, passion visualize
fire beneath the earth,
hot springs, glowing molten core fires
on earth harmonious

The ethers auric energy surrounding the body of each
living thing
the Unseen Forces, ancestors, angelic, elementals,
divas, wise ones
Christ light so lovingly present yet unseen but
sensed by many
by differing names yet all the same One
Source expression
Animal kingdom from domestic to
wild – fur, feather, fin scaled
and smooth ones; mammoths,
miniatures, all

All love expressed and encapsulating the light both
physically and spiritually
call it intuition, innate knowing, animal sense, all the
same life force
expressing itself from the original power of all-ness
Compassionate caring, sharing, creating
and sustaining
this and more are yours and all today
rejoice – celebrate your liveness
now and evermore

THE LIGHT

Out of the wilderness a step at a time
Each footfall comes closer to find
Out of the darkness, into the light
Blinded by fear, given new sight

    Some call "friend," others "Lord"
    Some unspoken still a holy sword
    Cutting asunder, the false from the true
    One divine spirit birthing a new you

The holy spirit flowing from the glorified one
Walking the wilderness until each heart is won
Some know the name, some know it not
All know the nature, Infinite light they've sought

    All to be found sooner or later
    All are imprinted with the ultimate fate
    Come from the shadows linger not there
    Come to the light where love you will share

Come my dearest, come forth today
No more wandering for pain will not pay
Come to the one who seeks you this hour
Come to the place of redeeming power

    Now is the moment for friendship divine
    Now is the moment for your soul to shine
    Joining in the peace, joy and everlasting love
    Remembering that which was forgotten
    Awakening to the light as a gentle dove

COSMIC CRUCIBLES OF LIGHT

All like little light bubbles floating in the sea of eternity
    Some on their Earth Walk
        others in the eternal ethers of higher vibration

Always consciously or unconsciously being a part of
generated light
    depending upon the quality of the thoughts,
    words, actions
        a refractory light generated from the intention
        of the heart

Light is pure consciousness – the ability to vibrate comes
from within
    wholly equipped with everything each living being needs
        pertaining to life, living in godliness

The ever-germinated life seed must grow
    exactly according to our beliefs
        being a fractal part of the One Divine Intelligence

We choose, sow, reap the product of our own experiences
    The light source always within us, dull or bright
        depending on where we place our intentional
        thoughts, or not

Always and forever the flow of light like roots of a tree
spreading wide
with vital alive vibrant nutrients rising throughout
the trunk
limbs, leaves, fruits, berries, blossoms up
into the crown
of glorious shade producing a fine canopy

As we arise to the source of all life
drawing nutrients of the same
magnificence caring within its flow
providing all that is needed to flourish

Spiraling up and out of the crown exploding in all directions
to the furthest reaches of the cosmos sweeping
downward in graceful treads of luminosity to
beyond the beyond
rising once more and then entering the root bed

As for humans up through grounded feet legs torso
midsection, organs, arms,
hands, back, spine, neck, face, head, enlivening
restoring, adjusting
all the details of each indivisible life
bringing forth the highest good radiating
out the crown
once more illuminating all space
with the glory
that is the Creator's love for all
living things

LIGHTEN UP

Laugh, learn to laugh, lighten up
Be happy, it's your life, make it a good one.
Rejoice! Rejoice! Rejoice!

Angels love to play with a happy heart
Angels come to laugh and stay
With one who has a joyous way

Angles come to a loving heart
To share the journey, joy impart
Angels shy away from gloom
One dark cloud, they leave the room

How much different are we than they
Joy attracts, woes repel, a sad mind
So, lift your light and let it shine
Let nothing keep you held behind

Strike out in joyous stride
And angels come alongside
Laugh and all heaven joins too
Joy is contagious; angels you'll woo

ILLUMINATING THE KINGDOMS

Illuminating the Kingdoms – human, animal, minerals, plants,
    elements of air, sky, water seas oceans aquifers rivers
    streams ponds,
        earth's surface and below, revitalizing
        precious topsoil
            all creatures upon the planet's surface

The mini and mammoth; those beneath the earth
    enriching with nutrients promoting more
        abundance of food, grasses trees
            varied green and growing things

Fire element within us and upon the earth
    Brought into harmonious balance
        these elements within all life air, water, fire,
            earth of which we each are created

Ethers, unseen but powerful sensed forces encompassed
in everything
    the mineral kingdom, angelic, elementals, divas,
        those unseen guardians, guides, wise ones,
            ascended masters, ancient ancestors

All touched by the loving energy that is available
to be shared by enlightened human hearts
eschewing darkness, thereby, may light
emanate from hearts and minds

Turning toward the increasing testimony of light
darkness then must fade as the original
true blueprint designed at the Dawn of Creation
each human life becoming ever more evident

How glorious, how privileged to be a small crucible
of potent potentiality contributing
to the enlightenment of every living organism
blessing and being blessed – Holy, Holy Light

WHAT SEASON BE IT?

"What season be it," ask the various fruit trees in the garden
A few glorious days in the 70s, warm yet a brisk breeze
Then days in 50s and 60s, out come the warmer clothes
The blessed always welcome rain to douse the earth
with moisture
Then a heat wave into the 80s and summer attire is needed

The fruit trees and other garden plants are confused
Is it winter, fall, spring or summer, a schizophrenic message
Of all the growing cycles divinely imparted to each living thing
The lemon tree bearing fruitage ripe, blossoms of fruit to come
Baby green lemons also adorning the old lemon tree

Roses having been severely pruned in winter while sap low
Showy new red leaves and vital stalks raising to the sky
The first buds of future glorious roses forming
All growing at once calling for spring to burst forth
The garden variety of plants and trees are so very confused

The light seems to shift daily
Global warming is manifesting
with thousands of evidential proofs

GARDEN GATE

I walk down a path to a garden gate so prettily framed with
an arbor of blooming roses. I gently open the gate and enter
this world of flowers, fauna, perfume, and the concerto
of songbirds.

There in the center of the garden sitting on a lovely bench
awaiting my arrival is the Divine Gardener.

Approaching with great awe and reverence in my heart.
We sit quietly for a few moments, observing my breathing,
watching colorful butterflies fluttering effortlessly from
plant to plant.

In the silence, His love envelops me, and I am touched and
comforted at a very deep level of my true being.

No words are needed here, for this one already knows my
heart and mind; I am fully known, fully heard, and
completely loved. Experiencing expansive peace and
comfort. Peace beyond my understanding ...

I linger in this radiant light, in this garden of my soul until
I am completely refreshed.

Preparing to leave, promising to return each day and
a mutual promise is given to me. If I come, this Radiant One
will meet me.

With solemn wonder, entering the world outside this blessed place. I am at ease and filled with quiet, unshakable strength, peace that passes all understanding from being alone with my comforter and my strength.

With great gratitude, knowing tomorrow I shall return and be greeted with unconditional love and understanding, and I shall return, and return, and return.

chapter 9

Holy Expectations

HOLY ANNUNCIATION

Have we missed a blessed or holy intended annunciation?
The visitor with the gifted seed to be embedded into the
awakening womb of one's own possibility?
Have we been absent from the golden promise of what
might have been or wants to be?
Being quiet enough to hear the rustling invitation
heretofore unknown is a necessary component
In the sweet, solitary silence, the presence gently enters this
chamber of contemplation,
welcomed with trusting expectancy of the ethereal visitor

Oh blessed seed of hope, to birth a beautiful long-awaited
promise incubating now within the heart
The pregnancy cherished, attended, held in the law of
secrecy until the creative power of birthing draws near
Once the light of life baptizes this special one now belonging
to the outer revealing visible world
no longer hidden in the sacred bowl of future promise,
exposing a new identity being brought forth into life
an energetic field all its own rippling sweetly into a larger
awaiting world

What destiny awaits ahead? What fate revealed by the
appearance of something fresh, vital, a new incarnation
The unknown is shown by the exposure to the flow of

creative power of the unseen divine union
The promise fulfilled in its own way and time granting this
privileged presence to find its way, one day at a time, as all must
There is no other revelatory journey centered in the
luminous Christ light available to all
The blessed annunciation of the Divine incarnation,
acknowledged heart by heart, soul by soul

Infinite intelligence enlivening every atom of all Creation

LIFE IS HAPPENING

Life is happening, don't you know?
Unseen perhaps but ever knowing
You plant a seed and under ground
The natural force its kind is growing

Life is happening, don't you know?
Unseen perhaps but ever sowing
Your thought held in mind and heart
Into your life its kind is showing

If you think love, love does surround
when you think hate, it does appear
You wonder why you're unhappy and sad
then betrayal from those you held dear

But in your heart, your secret mind
You held thoughts that were not kind
They must show up in your life, you see
For that is the law no force can bind

Cause and effect are the universal song
That which you think, you will reveal
That which you sow, you shall reap
There are no favorites in this deal

You choose the thoughts in your own mind
And mechanically they will dance your dance
You write the music which your song becomes
Be it a romantic waltz or an aggressive prance

Be it onto you according to your thoughts
What a human holds in consciousness shall be
Renew your mind with more loving forgiveness
And a new way of living, joy, peace you may see

It is up to you, it is up to me
No one can do it for us aright.
We are the star, director, and actor
The play reflects the script we write
What's happening is life; we are always the factor

EVERMORE

It is not the phrases and rhymes
  It is not the words, my dear
    It is the beating of your heart
      That causes the Unseen to hear

It is those moments in silence
  Spent alone with me
    The quieted mind and gentled heart
      That begins to see

To glimpse the spaces between spaces
  To see beyond the thin veil
    To hear knowledge you already knew
      But forgot in your travail

This is the moment of reconnection
  This is the moment of rebirth
    Born anew into multiple realities
      A space that brings sweet mirth

Joy is the evidence of work well done
  Peace is the evidence of inner connectedness
    The obvious drops away like unwanted burdens
      Riches from the soul is the spirit's
      blessedness

Come away, sweet beloved
  To the land of inner landscape
    Come away for a while each day
      Leaving any turmoil or strife

Trust the words that wish to enter
    Trust the source of your being
        Trust these fresh thoughts and prompting
           Trust your own hearts dream

Trust, listen, be silent and content for here is where
angels dwell
    Wander in the space where all, all is well
        Trust this is true substance that sustains,
           This is the place of evermore

THE MULTIPLICITY OF ONE

Back again after a wandering away
Back again to hear what you would say
I became discouraged with words
And wanted to see life at play

Speak with me, dear ones,
Ones of wisdom and perception
Speak to me of things
Beyond my knowing perception

We are here, pleased you wish to hear
We are always here, it is you that vacates our appointment
But that is not to blame or shame
But to assure you we are available always

In the multiplicity of one
You have seen the great mystery
The illusion of many and differing forms of life,
Yet in truth, all are just fractal realities, you see

Expressions will be forever unique and yet the same
The unlimited variety of color, shape, sound,
Yet of course, all emanating from the same universal source
The true divine intelligence with a thousand different names

The multiplicity of one comes in a 1000 Angel Faces
A 1000 multiplied by 1000 into infinity
There is no number, no limit, no lack of variety
That is the excitement of meeting each new human

Marvel at the uniqueness of this individual releasing
all thoughts of conformity
Celebrate the differences, the wide range of hues and sizes
Celebrate the languaging, the gestures, the ideas and speech
Celebrate creativity being exhibited in the multiplicity of One

WHO IS MY GOD?

Teaching about God, speaking of the Divine
Who is this of whom I speak?
Is there a personification or abstract?
Is there love or a retribution streak?

Is it the God of the Old Testament
With revenge, fiery brimstone?
Is it the gentle Jesus now the Christ
or is it an impersonal intelligence alone?

How can I surrender to the power and presence
within, when I am not totally clear
Who is the someone to whom I speak?
Is it someone I can trust or possibly fear?

How many mixed messages rattle within my brain
The God of my youth, the bible-thumping
fundamentalist version,
Or the expanded metaphysical divinity of oneness
The Love that permeates all and causes conversion?

Seeing this Unnamed One in nature so very clearly
In the majesty and beauty all around
Hearing the Divine in music that transports
The small voice within; is it you now found?

These are the questions that humankind asks
Wrestling with the God of their own understanding
And until this is settled at a deep level within,
No serenity or rest to calm the soul's reposing

Who is my higher power, my dearest friend
My guide, the origin of triumphant ones
Companion, teacher, beloved,
The one for whom my soul sweetly belongs

HOLY EXPECTATION

Why low energy when once overflowing stamina was
my portion?
Listening in the silence for understanding from the wise one
within
      Energy is key to all of life, and all living things!
      Energy is the fuel that runs the universal engine
          of constant movement in every form there is
          comes from Source, the originality of all Creation

Think of the cataclysmic eruptions during the forming
of Earth
      and even further reaching into the Cosmos
This creation and re-creation is happening still in the
outer reach
      of the known and unknown universal expanse

Draw closer to Source, centered in the flow of the energy
      that is ever abundant, free, available, ready
      to be channeled
      into the welcoming form.

Know all have access, thus act as if until you are
reinvigorated once more
Put more pep in your step, dance in the morning, use happy
talk and
      thoughts to surround yourself with the light energy
      that is as
      close as your next breath

The mind is the regulator, coming from old programing
adjust this and the flow will increase, eschew the inner
or verbal
      conversation of bemoaning low energy

What we think, speak, allow ourselves to believe, appears
This is the way of all of life, as we think, so we are
      Be excited about today and what may
      surprisingly appear,
      a holy expectation.

SWEET GIFT OF LIFE

Oh, sweet life, help me to savor thee
Oh, sweet life ever fresh, vital and new
May I always walk in the wonder of a child
In deep gratitude for the marvel of you

Oh, sweet life, fleeting and swift
How I drink your beauty each day
As I walk my chosen path of expression
Pondering what may come my way

Some days, the road winds upward
And I am wearied by the struggle I feel,
Others, I skip lightly upon earth's breast
Always in anticipation of what may reveal

Some days, the sky is gray and so am I,
Others, the Sun shines as I also do
Some, everything seems old and tired
Then those special days when all is new

Oh, sweet life, sweet gift to my soul
May I hold you in deepest reverence holy
Each sanctified breath a living prayer
Knowing each breath of life emanates from infinite substance

WHO AM I?

"Who am I?" The eternal question
Asked by humankind from beginning of time
Who am I? Why am I here?
Am I a special being or did we crawl out of the slime?

Who am I? What is this thing called me?
Do I have a purpose and will I find it?
Am I connected to all others and the Divine
Or a separate drifting thing, insignificant bit?

Am I special and will I do worthwhile things?
Is there someone listening to my laughter and tears?
Am I connected to the All in all?
Or am I confined to my own thoughts and fears?

Is there a hand that directs the tides
Is there One who holds back the sea
Is there an intelligence orchestrating it all
Is there One who knows all about me?

Am I a human being endeavoring to be spiritual?
Who is the One to help me with strife?
Am I a spiritual being having a human experience?
Where does one find the truth that shapes a life?

If I believe what others say, am I using my own mind?
If I listen but don't evaluate, how can I own what is mine?
If I read and study, but process not
Then all of my learning is nothing but rot!

Going within to hear that voice
So small and quiet that speak truth gently
When in deep listening my spirit quickens
I know then what's true for me, with a new light I see

No longer questioning who I am
I have found within a friend so true
Guiding, guarding and teaching me daily
Here I discover the I am, the ever new

I am that I am and that is surely enough
To love each day all of life as one possibly can
Asking to fnd your soul purpose authentically pure
Knowing now guided by that loving unseen hand

VIBRATIONAL ENERGY

Each has an energy that conducts a vibration
Each expresses what they believe inside
Each has a rhetoric of words, but if they match not
The result for them will surely hide

The belief and the vibration must be the same
Words can mask the true inner story
Changing one's own utterance or unuttered conversation
Can cause the vibrations to take on new glory

"Act as if until you are," is an old saying
Walk and talk like the thing you desire
Eventually it is attracted to you
Vibrational energy comes from inner fire

WELL OF INSPIRATION

I am here, you are here, we are here. Speak, friend and
Lord of My Soul

"In the depths there is a well of inspiration
bubbling with life's longing to be expressed
the pure stream of divine consciousness
awaits the emptied mind to receive unrepressed

Not always understanding
yet obedient to receive
so, the prophets of old
in their meditations were told

Visions given images of things to come,
no languaging to express the tools
Whirling insects like images
afraid to repeat and thought fools

The word spoken in silence
yet the word is true, always true
to the receptive soul
Simple one confounding the wise

Some who will live in silence
communing in sober response,

Some who come daily
will receive what Heaven knows

Come, dear one, do not forget
to sit in quiet; just be
I will stretch your hours, ease your work
if you will come and commune with me"

Thank you, Lord of my soul wisdom of all times,
nudge me to come desiring each moment
May I arise and meet with thee, walk, pray, read, write
creating this inspiring space within me

DESIRING

This emptiness rivets my gut like a whirlpool of downward
spiraling water
pulling me into its powerful retreat, retreat is what I do
hide, hiding, hidden where is the lady who was once a treat?
Where is the certainty, the laughter, the bubbling swagger,
where is that vision now in semi-fog, a stagger

Not even enjoying my own company, so lifeless
where is the glow, where did it go?
Feeling wounded, disappointed, same sadness known long ago
has surfaced again from a deep pool forgotten, hidden low
knowing too much to stay here in a somber silence

Even the garden gives only momentary delight,
Day and night I must find my way, a new way
just as the earth is searching for the new path
longing to see the dream that will make me laugh

Laugh with ecstasy, a sacred time in love's arms
singing joyously, dancing with wild ecstasy
the gift of being alive and finding a hidden self

Come beloved, come very soon
drowning in the darkness of my own tomb
hiding so long from honest view, desiring who?

THE UNSHARED LIFE

A life unshared is a shallow life
a life unobserved is a lonely plight
were we not created to walk two by two
so where is the one to come along side, calling you

Fate cannot be forced or made to act
but my patience is no longer intact
having dreamed, prayed, visualized and proclaimed
but still here alone and uncoupled in this game of life

No longer can I pretend that alone
Not liking to fend, for in truth,
it is becoming too heavy a burden to carry
slowly crumbling beneath its weight

"It is coming," for so long
having been told, that is almost more cruel
than being told "no" because then one wouldn't
hope, dream and wait

If the Universe within has shut the door
to fondest dreams then it is better to know
thereby ending the plight,
pretending to endure this lonely fight

Desiring help, but from whom and from where
Heaven has chosen to withhold answer
searching where does one go, but within
asking and speaking one's own soul truth

So, dear one, in downward spiral
hold on, knowing take the ride
you will survive and life will once again
become harmonious within your stride

You will again walk your walk
with confidence and joy
feeling your way each and every day
joyous with what is and what is not

PONDERING ON EGO

The ego is not the enemy, but an ally when trained
    untrained it is self will run riot—
        more, more, me, me, mine, mine, etc

Ego desires to feel important demands to be right
    The trained ego takes the positive strengths,
        charm, intellect, creativity, and channels these
          inherent gifts into the greater expression
          of the collective good,
            not just personal desires

Now seeing how ego in its intended use, is a gifted ally
    to live life successfully for oneself and others –
        family, business, community, tribe or out into
          the expansive world in subtle or profound ways

The ego can be cause or it can be effect
    The trained mind is much more powerful than
        the untrained or uneducated mind
          All actions have reactions throughout the
          ethers of the universe

No word or thought or prayer is unnoticed,
    all vibrate at a frequency heard and felt by the
        originality of it all even though
          we may be unaware consciously

May Grace rule your days and nights,
    your thoughts and dreams
        May each breath you take move the energies
          toward the light of loving expression
           This is surely a worthy work

DIVINE UNFOLDING

Awakening with a heavy pall upon ones being
    Weighted feeling in the morning
    as if in heavy sleep, a semi numbness?
Like crawling into conscious movement entering a new life
    A chrysalis awakening swimming in wet stuff,
    a semi-sedated, not yet butterfly

Endeavoring to unfurl, uncurl folded wings unfamiliar body
    Ah, to be a newly created butterfly
    drying oneself in the sun
Experimenting with unfamiliar yet embedded knowledge
    of how to stretch,
    flutter and finally fly

Antennas sensing the air, a light breeze and sounds of nature
    Hungry? Thirsty? What, Where? How?
    Ancient wisdom arising, gently whispering
 A response or nudge for each honest inquiry
    The eyes searching,
    pondering in the glory of the day
Colors, shapes, blue so high above
    Can it be reached?

Curiosity is the gift of exploration into a once familiar
    now expanding world, energy arising as life force awakens
Each cell, molecule, pulsating in this delicate form from
    thinking mechanism, hearing, senses, smell, taste
The bodily fluids flowing impulses so true as to where to
satisfy thirst,
    hunger, and the need for nectar to be sought and found

Are there others?
    A colony?
Feeling the breeze now ruffling wings, flight is engaged
    A radiant sight, awakened, awake, a new metaphor
in the magnificent creative genius of the Divine unfolding
    What is true in nature is true for humanity

THE VEIL HAS PARTED

So lightly does the veil part
And accepts the one with loving hands
Who casting off the garments of the Earth
Unto more celestial and peaceful lands

That veil between realities so thin
We live as if it does not exist in time
And when the opening is for us
So quietly the passage that will be thine

In saying farewell, never goodbye
To cherished family and friends dear
In remembering the eternality of life
And we will again see those once here

The tears that may run down a face
This seemingly sad day will fade
And joy again will be a way of recalling
All the lovely joy we made

For we shall see them as they truly are
And they see us no longer through diffused glass
For in the clarity of celestial light
We all with helping, loving hands will pass

So, for today Dear One, bidding you farewell
And some tomorrow unknown to me
That long passage of light will call
And from Earth's journey, shall be free

Free at last, free at last
Into the place from where all are lovingly created
By the one sweet, divine energy of compassion
Returning to past beloveds, sorrow now abated

THE SEARCH FOR THE BELOVED

Why need I search for the Beloved?
To where could I travel, in what land look?
But upon the dear faces resplendent with life
Here is the wonder of love unforsaken

Each child, grandchild, and great grandchild dear
Is an expression of the Beloved to me
Why search for and wander up and down
When all is right here if we but see

The past is a fascinating story
The future, a fantastic trip
But to be in the now is glory and wonder
perhaps a paradoxical trick?

acknowledgments

JERRY WAYNE DOWNS is a prolific and imaginative artist who uses many differing expressions—futuristic worlds, portraits, commission pieces, land and seascapes, surrealism, and also romantic dreamlike atmospheres, all ripping through the veil of conventionality, and prompting questions about the fragility of our present. A former animator for Disney, his experience and style bring enchantment to his works.

JerryDowns44@gmail.com

GAIL RIENA MICHAEL is an editor, author and poet who encourages and assists writers as they ready their books for release. She has published her own books and poetry and is a co-author in the *Giving Gratitude...Wake Up Live the Life You Love Series.*

Capri383@gmail.com

JULIE SUTTERHOLM is an artist known for her brilliant enameled tree of life sculptures coupled with female figures. She has recently segued to setting enameled "stones" into jewelry and wall pieces. Julie works in copper, steel and bronze medias using an oxy-acetylene torch to create pieces both functional and artistic. She is a popular and well-collected artist in Laguna Beach, California, and exhibits at the Sawdust Festival summer and winter venues.

copperfeel8008@gmail.com

about Patricia

Patricia Truman has presented us with another soulful and insightful book of poetry, *Roses in the Lemon Tree*, a dedication to her beloved mother.

After many years of writing published articles in newspapers and meditations for *Creative Thought* Magazine, she released her first book in 2022, *Mystic Cloud Walker*.

Patricia, an ordained minister, was a speaker and prayer practitioner for Centers for Spiritual Living where she taught classes and performed ceremonies and Sacred Circles. She is also a successful businesswoman who has been given many awards throughout her 42+ year career. Her most cherished is the 2008 Realtor of the Year award which was an acknowledgement of being held in high esteem by her peers. As an escrow officer, she was pivotal in the success of helping start an escrow company. She is also a personal investor and active community supporter.

She has a robust and growing family which includes ten grandchildren, twenty-one great-grands, and two great-great-grands. With her ever-growing tribe who she dearly loves, she relishes being a mentor and supporter to all, a soul-satisfying experience.

Patricia recalls, as a child, her mother tending the garden as the roses wrapped themselves around the lemon tree amid her flowering plants. She learned from her mother the lessons that the earth and her garden had to teach. These are some of the reflections in this beautiful and insightful book.

Patricia also enjoys friends, family, traveling, walking, yoga and the beauty of her lovely Laguna Beach community, her home and garden.

facebook: www.facebook.com/patriciapepertruman
website: patriciatruman.com

www.ingramcontent.com/pod-product-compliance
Lightning Source LLC
Chambersburg PA
CBHW060909120626
46553CB00001B/256